PRAISE FOR *LET HOPE IN*

"I feel like Pete Wilson writing about hope is like Max Lucado writing about grace. It reads like a conversation with a friend who has been down the road you're on and knows which potholes to avoid and which vistas not to miss."

— **Jon Acuff**
New York Times Best-selling
Author of *Start*

"After reading this once, I quickly knew that my copy would become well-worn. Pete tells the truth in such a profound, yet relatable way, giving practical choices that will bring true healing and freedom to so many. *Let Hope In* is a powerful reminder that God can redeem and transform any situation, and that change really is possible."

— **Natalie Grant**
Gospel Music's 5-Time
Female Artist of the Year
Grammy-Nominated
Recording Artist

"With all the hurt and pain in the world today, people are hungry to hear the message of hope found in the good news of the Gospels. In *Let Hope In,* my friend Pete Wilson challenges you to make the practical choices that will set you free. Stop living as a prisoner of your past and read this book today!"

— **Rick Warren**
Founding Pastor,
Saddleback Church
Author of *The Purpose
Driven Life*

"Pete Wilson is a master communicator with a gift for encouraging hurting people with just the right words. *Let Hope In* is a brilliant look at the healing and growth we can all experience in Christ. I seriously love this book and I'm so thankful Pete wrote it. I can't wait to share it with others and see the healing this book points us to!"

— **Jud Wilhite**
Senior Pastor, Central
Christian Church
Author of *Pursued*

"Hope is one of the most powerful things in the world. With it there is not a problem that cannot be conquered, a relationship that cannot be restored, or a burden that cannot be lifted. However, we seem to live in a world that attacks the thought of having hope by consistently feeding us with information on how bad things are . . . and how bad things are going to be. I am so glad that Pete wrote this book to help us shift our thinking from how bad things can be to how good things can be, and how if we switch our thinking to making better choices that our lives will be flooded with hope unlike anything we've ever experienced."

— **Perry Noble**
Senior Pastor, NewSpring
Church

"It is impossible to live fully without hope. Yet, so many are trying to live without it. Pete Wilson writes with compassion and confidence that every person may experience a new beginning in Christ and live with the confidence and expectation that the future is in His Hands. I highly recommend this very practical and helpful book."

— **Jack Graham**
Pastor, Prestonwood Church

"In my more than twenty years of working with hurting people, I've seen old wounds tear families apart more times than I can count. Some tragedy or mistake in the past totally derails their life and puts them in a downward spiral of guilt, shame, fear and regret. In *Let Hope In*, Pete Wilson tackles our old hurts head-on, showing us a biblical, practical process for letting go of old wounds and moving forward into a new future."

— **Dave Ramsey**
New York Times Best-selling
Author
Nationally Syndicated Radio
Show Host

"Pete Wilson doesn't just write about hope—he embodies it. These are the choices that God uses to bring hope to you. I wouldn't miss it!"

— **John Ortberg**
Senior Pastor, Menlo Park
Presbyterian Church
Author of *Who Is This Man*?

"Read this book armed with a highlighter, Bible, and box of tissues. You will want to highlight several dozen great insights. You'll want to read for yourself the Bible stories Pete presents. And the tissues? We all get emotional when hope comes in. Prepare yourself for tears of joy."

— **Max Lucado**
Pastor and Best-selling
Author

"Pete Wilson is the real deal. His life and ministry points you and me to a tangible hope available to us all. If you've ever felt like an unlikely candidate for hope in the present because of mistakes in the past, then welcome to the club. We're all there. Pete's latest book—and more importantly, the life he leads—points us to a God who loves unlikely candidates, bringing hope to those who might describe themselves or their situations as 'hopeless'. In the Kingdom of God, hopeless isn't a word that exists. Don't believe me? Then, *Let Hope In*."

— **Jeff Henderson**
Lead Pastor, Gwinnett
Church

LET
HOPE
IN

LET HOPE IN

4 Choices That Will Change Your Life
Forever

PETE WILSON

W PUBLISHING GROUP

AN IMPRINT OF THOMAS NELSON

Published in Nashville, Tennessee, by W Publishing Group. W Publishing is a registered trademark of Thomas Nelson, Inc.

Pete Wilson is represented by The A Group, a full-service marketing, technology, and brand development company in Brentwood, Tennessee. Learn more at www.AGroup.com.

Thomas Nelson, Inc., titles may be purchased in bulk for educational, business, fund-raising, or sales promotional use. For information, please e-mail SpecialMarkets@ ThomasNelson.com.

Unless otherwise noted, Scripture quotations are taken from *Holy Bible*, New Living Translation (NLT). © 1996, 2004, 2007. Used by permission of Tyndale House Publishers, Inc., Wheaton, Illinois 60189. All rights reserved.

Scripture quotations marked NIV are taken from the Holy Bible, New International Version®, NIV®. © 1973, 1978, 1984, 2011 by Biblica, Inc.™ Used by permission of Zondervan. All rights reserved worldwide. www.zondervan.com.

Scripture quotations marked MSG are taken from *The Message* by Eugene H. Peterson. © 1993, 1994, 1995, 1996, 2000, 2001, 2002. Used by permission of NavPress Publishing Group. All rights reserved.

Scripture quotations marked AMP are taken from Amplified® Bible, © 1954, 1958, 1962, 1964, 1965, 1987 by The Lockman Foundation. Used by permission.

Scripture quotations marked NASB are from the NEW AMERICAN STANDARD BIBLE®, © The Lockman Foundation 1960, 1962, 1963, 1968, 1971, 1972, 1973, 1975, 1977, 1995. Used by permission.

Scripture quotations marked NKJV are from THE NEW KING JAMES VERSION. © 1982 by Thomas Nelson, Inc. Used by permission. All rights reserved.

Library of Congress Control Number: 2013911625

ISBN 978-0-8499-6456-5

Printed in the United States of America

13 14 15 16 17 RRD 5 4 3 2 1

To my wife, Brandi—
You truly are my solace in the storm.
I've never loved you more fully and
needed you more deeply.

CONTENTS

CONTENTS

I pray that the eyes of your heart may be enlightened in order that you may know the hope to which he has called you.

—**Ephesians 1:18** NIV

CHOICE ONE:
CHOOSING TO TRANSFORM INSTEAD OF TRANSFER

1

TRANSFORM OR TRANSFER

I do some of my best dreaming with my boys. We love to sit in our screened-in porch off the back of our house and just talk. Recently, I proposed the question I often do with them regarding the future. "What do you guys want to be when you grow up?" I love asking my boys this because it changes about once a month and is usually dependent on the last movie they've watched.

My youngest, Brewer, went first. "I want to be a policeman," he said boldly.

My middle son, Gage, took a little more time to think before he sheepishly said, "I think I might want to be a teacher like Pee-Paw."

Then Jett, my oldest, said, "Dad, I want to be an NFL football player. What I can't figure out, though, is whether I'll play in college or if I'll just skip college and go straight to the NFL."

We sat there for a second just staring at each other when Brewer looked at me and asked, "Dad, do you think you'll still be a pastor when you grow up?"

For a moment I forgot about reality and enjoyed having a blank slate from which to dream.

I love the idea of not being "grown up" yet. In my mind that means I still have more ahead of me than behind me. It means I can dream without all the restrictions of reality that comes along with getting older. It means it is still possible for me to become the person I really want to become.

I think most of us are pretty hopeful about the future. We carry our dreams around believing that one day we'll give birth to them. We generally believe that tomorrow is going to be better than today. We like to think that our careers will head in the right direction, our relationships will become even richer, and that the sense of purpose we're chasing after will finally be fulfilled.

But there's one thing often standing in the way of this desirable future we all hope and long for: our seemingly unforgettable past.

The reality is that the best predictor of our future is, in fact, our past. What we have done in the past is probably what we will do in the future, unless there have been some big changes, some monumental transformation.

And I want to start by asking important questions: Do you like who you're becoming? Who you're growing up to be? Really?

IS YOUR PAST YOUR PAST?

I first met Kim at the church that I pastor in Nashville. She was waiting to speak to me after one of the weekend worship experiences when I saw her eyes. While I happily continued somewhat meaningless small talk with a few people, I was eager to hear what she wanted to talk about. I could tell her heart was heavy and that she was about to explode if she didn't talk to someone soon.

Our conversation was surprisingly quick and unemotional, but she made it clear that she needed to sit down and talk as soon as possible. I felt God prompting me to make it happen quickly.

We soon found time to meet, and similar to our last brief encounter, it was clear that Kim was ready to get down to business.

"My life is a wreck," she blurted out.

My first admittedly insensitive thought was, *Well, join the club.* The reality is nobody usually asks to meet with a pastor because they want to share how pleasant life is.

She continued, "I'm sure you hear a lot of crazy stuff, but I need you to know before I share with you that I really am a good person. I mean, I'm not good, but I love God and I want to do the right thing, but I screw up so often."

My experience is that it takes most people longer to set up their confession than it takes to actually confess. Kim, however, eventually got around to pouring out her heart. It turns out that she had made some really poor relationship choices over the past year and a half. She had been involved sexually with three different men, two of which had been married at the time of her relationship with them.

She was sorry, broken, repentant.

But she was also confused.

She sobbed, "Why do I keep doing this? Why do I keep hurting myself and the people around me? Why? Why?"

While this statistic is unsubstantiated, I would guess that I have no answer for 90 percent of the questions that are asked in my office. Sure, I've got guesses and opinions, but after eighteen years of ministry, I have to admit that I often feel more lost today than when I started.

But as Kim and I continued to talk that day, there was a major theme that emerged: her past.

Kim had spent a good portion of her life trying to win her father's attention, his approval, and ultimately, his love. She shared with me story after story of how she fell short of his expectations and failed to show up on his radar.

Interestingly enough, Kim's first affair was with her boss. As we talked about that relationship, I learned that it started because he was simply kind, understanding, and genuinely concerned about her. These were all qualities she wished her father would have had.

> What happened in our past, if not dealt with properly, is more than likely crippling us from becoming who we were created to become.

Now don't misunderstand me: I'm not trying to excuse the decisions that followed. I'm not trying to pin this on her father. I just want to point out that we can't deny the role her past wounds were playing in her current decisions.

A heartrending thing about us humans is that we seem to be hardwired to replay the past—especially when our past includes pain and disappointment. We all have natural inclinations and, at times, compulsions to allow our past to deeply impact our present.

And your past is not your past if it's still impacting your present.

Ever wonder why we make a handful of New Year's resolutions every year but rarely keep them? And if we do, we almost never see a lasting change?

Ever wonder why we keep repeating the same mistakes over and over?

Ever wonder why we have such a difficult time maintaining healthy relationships?

Of course you have. We all have.

Is it because we're not disciplined enough? Is it because we don't want it bad enough? While the answer to either of those questions could obviously be yes, I think it's much deeper than that.

When we keep struggling with the gnawing question of "Why am I not getting what I want in life?" one of the questions behind it may be "What am I still carrying with me from my past?"

Whether our pain is close to the surface or hidden deep within our hearts, what happened in our past, if not dealt with properly, is more than likely crippling us from becoming who we were created to become.

But the good news is, who we were yesterday doesn't have to limit who we can be today!

Some of my most popular messages over the years have been on loving others. I'm not sure I have ever met someone who didn't want to love others more radically.

I believe many people listen to these messages on love with hopes of being inspired to live a life of "love." And trust me, I know how to deliver messages that inspire people to love more. But I'm afraid there's a deeper problem.

While many of us have been inspired to love more and have set our hearts on loving more, some of us, in fact, fail miserably when it comes to loving more. The problem is not inspiration. The problem is not what I call "want to." The problem is, we may not have the wholeness to love and live the way we want to.

I'm learning that everyone needs healing. Everyone has been hurt. Some of us have been hurt worse than others, but no one escapes this life without some emotional bruising along the way. And if we haven't dealt with the hurt from our past, it will continue to impact everything we touch.

In other words: *If we don't learn to transform the pain, we'll just transfer it.*

Your secret sin nobody knows about.

The broken marriage you went through.

The sexual abuse you suffered.

The surprise divorce your parents got.

The miscarriage you experienced.

The bully who made your freshman year miserable.

Your overbearing, critical parent.

Any or all of these things can and most usually will have a tremendous impact on our lives. If we don't find ways to learn from our past, we will almost always be doomed to repeat it.

> **If we don't learn to transform the pain, we'll just transfer it.**

Maybe what's going on in your life is you're seeking healing for what is still an open wound. Maybe you're longing for the sewing up of something that has long remained ripped and ragged.

Awareness of our past doesn't always come easy. What does come easy is denial. We are quick to intentionally bury emotions that make us feel ashamed or uncomfortable. We confuse what we're feeling with what we think or have been told we should be feeling.

To complicate matters further, there tends to be a pervasive attitude in some circles of the church that communicate that once you give your life to Christ, once you've become a Christian, you at least need to act like you've got it all together.

Read your Bible.

Wear your mask.

Put your best foot forward.

Look happy.

But whatever you do: Don't be a whiner. Don't ask questions. Don't be a pain. Don't be a burden.

I'm not sure where this attitude comes from, but I think it originates with fear. We don't want people to share their broken dreams, hurts, or pain because we're afraid we won't have all the answers.

Is it possible we're afraid that God won't be able to really heal us?

Are we afraid that admitting pain and brokenness somehow discounts our salvation experience? If when we put our faith and trust in Jesus—the old becomes new—why don't we feel new? Why don't we feel transformed? Are we praying wrong?

BUT GOD

One of my favorite stories in the Bible is the account of Joseph. Talk about a tumultuous past.

Joseph was the youngest of twelve boys. It's tough being the youngest, isn't it? My youngest, Brewer, is six and has one goal in life. Well, actually two. The first one is to be able to accurately hit the toilet while standing up to pee. But his main goal in life is getting his two older brothers to acknowledge him. He watches everything they do and follows them from activity to activity. So whether it's playing PlayStation, wrestling in the living room, or competing in a game of touch football in the front yard, Brewer is going to be in the middle of it. And nothing, I mean nothing, brings a bigger smile to his face than when his older brothers invite him into their world.

Joseph was favored by his father, which put him at obvious odds with the rest of his brothers. They were filled with incredible jealousy toward him. They beat him up, threw him into a pit, sold him into slavery, and pretended he was dead.

That would be a devastating series of events for any young person, but imagine all of that happening by the hand of your own brothers from whom you crave love and acceptance. Can you imagine how devastating that moment must have been as he looked up from the pit, broken and bruised, only to see the face of his brothers laughing at him?

It's funny how when someone says they love you, you can't really feel it, but when someone says or shows they "don't love you anymore," you feel every ounce of it draining out of your entire being.

The rejection of his brothers would just be the beginning for Joseph. He would go on to be falsely accused of rape and thrown into prison where he spent day after day wondering where things went wrong, wondering why his brothers hated him. Why had his past been so full of injustice?

Through a remarkable series of events, not only was Joseph released from prison, but he eventually rose to second in command over all of Egypt.

While Joseph was helping lead Egypt, the country endured a vicious drought that forced his brothers to travel to him seeking food for their families. It's a long story, but eventually not only was Joseph reunited with his brothers, but he also forgave them. In a powerful moment, he looked them in the eyes and said, "You meant evil against me, *but God* meant it for good" (Gen. 50:20 NASB, emphasis mine).

Another way of putting it is, you meant harm, but God had a different plan. Joseph didn't try to deny the past. He didn't pretend that his brothers had never hurt him deeply. But he has the grace to grieve it rather than transfer it.

I love the phrase "but God" and believe a case could be made that it's one of the most important phrases in the entire Bible. This phrase is used throughout Scripture as a turning point, a line of demarcation between peril and rescue, chaos and control, fall and redemption, hurt and healing.

But God! Every time I read a verse that says "but God," it is fantastically good news. There are literally hundreds of verses that have "but God" in both the Old and New Testaments:

The psalmist in Psalm 73:26: "My health may fail, and my spirit may grow weak, *but God* remains the strength of my heart; he is mine forever."

Jesus in Matthew 19:26: "Humanly speaking, it is impossible. *But with God* everything is possible."

The apostle Paul in Acts 13:29–30: "When they had done all that the prophecies said about him, they took him down from the cross and placed him in a tomb. *But God* raised him from the dead!"

Once we were dead in sin, *but God* made us alive! Once we were captive to our past, *but God* made us free! Once we were unworthy, *but God* has promised to spend eternity unwrapping the riches of his grace in kindness toward us!

There's no way around the past. No matter how hard you try, you can't erase it. The goal here is not to become a person who doesn't have a history—that's impossible and useless. The goal is to find a new way of working with the past so it does not continue to impact our future. The goal is to fight the inner urge we all have to return to the past.

ANYTHING IS POSSIBLE

At our church we say, "Everyone is welcome, because nobody is perfect, but anything is possible." I really believe that. I believe that no matter what you've done, where you've been, no matter how far you feel from God today, we worship a God of open arms. A God who says everyone is welcome.

Not only do I believe that "everyone's welcome, because nobody's perfect," I'm also relentlessly committed to the idea that "anything's possible." And I think you may be too. Perhaps it's why you picked up this book. You know that transformation in your life is possible. You know that healing is possible. There's some-

God is bigger than your history and more concerned with your destiny.

thing inside of you that says there's more to this existence here on this earth. You long to become the man or woman God created you to be when he thought you into existence.

We love to cheer for the underdog and believe in our core that every life makes a difference. And we are right. There is no one God can't use and no one whose bro-kenness is too broken for God. We know this is true for our friends when we want to encourage them. Yet, when it comes to the places of our innermost sense of shame and regret, we often wonder if it is really true that God can work all things together for good for those who love him.

This is what you need to know going into a future that you desperately hope will be different: from the very moment human-ity fell into sin, God's plan, God's passion, has been to redeem us and restore us to the life for which we are made.

God is bigger than your history and more concerned with your destiny.

This act of grace, this act of forgiveness, this act of restoration God wants to give. It cannot be forced.

Like anything from God, it has to be received like a gift freely, willfully, and intentionally. This book is about how we receive this gift God so willingly desires to give to us. This book is about dreaming again. This book is about learning to transform the pain so we no longer transfer it.

In the chapters that follow, we will be exploring how many of our choices in life and relationship are tied to our past. Our goal is to break the hold the past has over us, keep what is useful, but also confront the things that limit our ability to live the life God created us to live. And so begins the journey—a journey that you've wanted to take for a very long time, a journey toward hope.

2

LEAVING SHAME BEHIND

When Will Porter was just eight years old, his life was good. He spent his days playing on the playground, fishing, and enjoying friends as every little boy should. He grew up in an upper-class home where he was blessed to have everything he needed and most things he wanted.

His parents had enrolled him in one of the best schools around. Will says he still remembers the day his school hired a new choir director. This was a big deal because Will, like many of his friends, loved being a part of the choir.

This new choir director came with an impressive résumé. Everyone in the small community of Easton, Maryland, was elated that their kids would get the opportunity to be mentored by someone of his caliber.

As everyone expected, the director took the choir to new heights. Before long, Will and the other boys had the privilege of performing across the country. Everyone knew the credit went to the new choir director. What everyone didn't know is that every time the director was alone with young Will, the director would molest him.

Will recalls, "From the first time he touched me, I knew it was wrong. It was a touch I knew was different from any other touch. I was instantly full of confusion and guilt. And that touch, that happened for years, can still bring pain into my life today. He would abuse me at least once a week for the next seven years of my life."

Will also remembers the day they had just returned from a long choir tour. "As our bus pulled into the parking lot, there were five police cars waiting for us. I instantly thought about what had been going on with the choir director. The police came onto the bus, put handcuffs on our choir director, put him in the back of the police car, and drove off. I was scared. I was scared to death. I thought I would be next. I feared they would take me off to jail as well."

Will stepped off the bus, not saying a word to anyone. His parents escorted him to the car and they headed for home. His mother would eventually break the silence by asking, "Were you involved in that in any way?" Will realized later that his mom was just trying to check on him, but he was a panicked little kid who thought he was in trouble. So he quickly responded, "No, Mom, I wasn't."

It was never mentioned again in Will's family.

Will spent the rest of his growing-up years trying to hide the secret. So by his freshman year of high school he was getting in all kinds of trouble. Will started to mimic the abuse he had experienced from the choir director by experimenting sexually with girls. He also started to abuse alcohol to try to numb the constant pain.

His parents, realizing that something was wrong, decided to send him off to a boarding school. One day Will heard his name called over the intercom. The head priest wanted to see him in his apartment. Will reluctantly showed up, sure he was in trouble for something he had done.

Will recounts, "As soon as I sat down in the priest's apartment, he offered me a drink. Before I even realized what was going on, it all started again. That was probably the lowest I've ever been in my life. I learned how to just switch things off so I had no feeling. He abused me over and over. Each time it was like I was dead, just laying there."

Will was haunted by questions: *Why? What did I do? Does God hate me? Do I like this? Is this who I am? Why am I constantly a target?*

He went on to college, got married, and had three kids, all the while working extremely hard to cover up the deep shame he had from his childhood.

OUR HISTORY

Shame is the heart disease of every era. People are dying from it—some quickly, others slowly.

In its simplest definition, shame is the deep sense that you are unacceptable because of something you did or something that was done to you.

Shame is not like guilt. Guilt says, "I did something wrong," while shame says, "I am wrong." Guilt is the person who says, "I'm responsible, I messed up, I was wrong," and they expect punishment and need forgiveness. Shame is the person who thinks they don't belong because of something that they did or something that has been done to them.

Shame says you're not normal. You stick out and if people find out, you'll be kicked out.

Shame has no prejudices or preferences; it impacts each and every one of us. It doesn't matter who you are; it targets anyone and everyone.

And so our human response to shame is almost always the same and can be summed up in one word: hide.

We believe the message of our past is clear: we have fallen short; we don't measure up.

Other people are acceptable; we are not.

They succeed; we fail.

They are good; we are bad.

They are important; we are disposable.

The voices of our past have all confirmed that, and it's easy to think that God himself joins those many voices, even though he certainly does not.

When it comes to faults, failures, or screwups from our past, the reality is we're quick to want to cover up, to want to deny, to avoid, to want to blame someone else.

We work really hard to shake off the feeling of shame by minimizing and covering stuff up.

> We work really hard to shake off the feeling of shame by minimizing and covering stuff up.

The Bible has a lot to say about shame and its remedy. In fact, I believe it is a general theme of the Bible as a whole. We read in Genesis 2:25 that "the man and his wife were both naked, but they felt no shame." Our story as humans started off so well. In our first chapter, there was absolutely no shame, with people walking around naked literally and figuratively—nakedness without shame, fully known and fully loved. I know this is ancient history, but it's important for us to understand that this is where our story began.

The Bible tells us that God created an amazing place called the garden of Eden. This would be a place for Adam and Eve to enjoy God's creation, find their purpose, and spend time getting to know their Creator.

There was really only one rule or guideline. God made it clear to both Adam and Eve that they were not to eat the fruit from the tree in the center of the garden.

The Serpent came along and tried to convince Eve there wouldn't be any consequences to not following God's wisdom. Eve saw how beautiful and delicious the fruit looked and was convinced it would be okay. So she ate it and also gave some to Adam, who ate it with her.

The writer of Genesis tells us "at that moment their eyes were opened, and they suddenly felt shame at their nakedness. So they sewed fig leaves together to cover themselves" (v. 3:7).

Later when they heard God, they hid. And then God called out to Adam, "Where are you?" (v. 9)

Adam replied, "I heard you walking in the garden, so I hid. I was afraid because I was naked" (v. 10).

And just like that, shame is woven into the very fabric of all our stories. Welcome to a story where shame has been part of the air we breathe almost from the beginning.

Shame says I'm unpresentable. I'm unpresentable to the people around me (I must cover up my nakedness) and, even more devastating, I'm unpresentable to God (I must hide in the garden).

This shame prompts Adam and Eve to fashion masks from leaves in order to hide what was true about them. That day all humanity learned how to look over our shoulders, how to say one thing and mean another, how to hide fear and deceit behind a fake smile.

We feel this sense of exposure and shame as though we've been found out that we're not who we're supposed to be. It has created a lot of habits for us. It's why we keep secrets. It's why we can put on facades and pretend we're someone we're not.

We learned how to respond to the question, "How are you?"

with "I'm fine." But deep down we know this isn't true. We're not fine. We're not fine at all.

In reality, we are hurting, lonely, confused, frightened.

So we hop from book to book, seminar to seminar, church to church, looking for that new technique promising to help us change. It may be the very reason that you picked up this particular book. Perhaps you're even thinking, *I've heard all of this before.* But do we really want to change or just appear as though we're attempting to change? In reality, most of us are probably okay with just the appearances. Or maybe we're afraid we can't change. Either way, we continue to put ourselves in situations where healing *could* happen, but our desire to hide is greater than our desire to change.

INTO THE LIGHT

One of my favorite tasks around the house is vacuuming. I don't know exactly why, but few things bring me more satisfaction than seeing the clean lines in a carpet when I'm done.

A similar household task that doesn't bring me as much satisfaction is sweeping the floor. I hate sweeping the kitchen because whenever you sweep the floor, as much as you can try to collect all the dirt in one place, when you sweep it into the dust pan, you always end up with that little line of dirt right there at the edge of the pan. You know what I'm talking about.

You sweep and you sweep and you sweep. You try a different broom, you come at it from a new angle, but it doesn't matter. That little line of dirt is always still there, just laughing at you and taunting you.

I learned recently that there's actually a word for that little line of dirt. It's called a "frust." Seriously, try googling it. It's a combination of the words *frustration* and *dust,* and it leads to paralyzing frustration and deep agony.

There's only one thing you can do with frust. I carefully sweep it into the living room where we have a large area rug, and when nobody is looking, I lift up the corner of the area rug and, as cliché as it sounds, give the frust a violent push with my broom and it disappears under there, never to be seen again (except maybe the next time I lift up the corner to sweep more under there).

Now while that may work with frust, I promise you it doesn't work with shame. And yet, isn't that exactly what most of us try to do?

Shame in our lives and the way we deal with it is often like frust. We try all sorts of ways to sweep it up and clear it out, even if it means we just resort to sweeping it under the rug, hoping no one will ever find it. But it's always there.

Nothing— and I mean nothing— makes us feel lonelier than our secrets.

Nothing—and I mean nothing— makes us feel lonelier than our secrets.

This is exactly what happened to my friend Will. He continued to hide the shame from his past, but that just led Will to develop a self-destructive, hidden lifestyle. That hidden lifestyle was destroying everything that meant something to him, and unfortunately, this is all too common for someone full of shame. People with shame don't believe they deserve anything good. In many ways, they sabotage everything of value to them.

It really doesn't make a lot of sense. You would think that anyone and everyone would jump at the chance to rid themselves of shame. Yet, far too many times I've seen this play out in my own life. Shame deceptively but convincingly leads us to believe that we deserve to be shackled to it for the rest of our life. We believe we don't deserve to be free of shame.

Shame leads us to so many unhealthy extremes.

Will and I are neighbors and struck up a friendship. He was doing such a great job of hiding, I had no clue about his past. I felt there was some kind of wall there, but I just couldn't put my finger on it. Over time, he and his family started attending the church I pastor and then joined a community group Bible study my wife and I lead in our home. The more involved Will got, the more he wanted to ask for help, but fear usually won out and he stayed silent.

One thing Will would do to escape the stress of his hidden life was exercise incessantly. One day he was at the gym and had been on the treadmill for well over an hour when a guy walked by and jokingly asked, "What are you running from, man?" Will knew he was joking but as the guy walked away, he hit the stop button on the treadmill and just stood there, repeating the question under his breath. "What are you running from, Will?"

A few weeks later, Will did one of the most courageous things I've ever seen in a community group: he told his story. He shared from his heart not only what had happened to him in his past but how his shame had led him to a dark, hidden life that was destroying his marriage.

I was so proud of Will that night. It was the beginning of a new life for him—a life where he would be free from the shackles of shame, which had dominated so much of his life.

The shame that was so powerful while it was in the dark was now being exposed and weakened by the light.

UNDESERVED LOVE

One of the more interesting stories in the Bible is the unique love story of Hosea and Gomer. Outside of the cross of Jesus Christ, I don't know of a better picture in the Bible of God's radical grace, love, and forgiveness than the one captured in this crazy story.

This story is not just about Hosea and Gomer; it's about the troubled marriage between God and his people. Throughout the Bible, marriage is used as a metaphor to describe our relationship with God.

The story of the prophet Hosea and his troubled marriage is a powerful testimony to us not only of our own tendency to be unfaithful to God but also of God's passionate love for us. The precise details of Hosea's troubled marriage are sketchy, and we are left to fill in some of the details with our imagination. But here are the basic facts along with some of the background information required. I've split the story into four acts for simplicity.

ACT 1: God gives Hosea, a prophet in the Old Testament, the unusual command to marry the prostitute Gomer. Yes, she is a prostitute and her name is Gomer. Two strikes. This was the first time and the last time we're aware of God giving any such instructions. But Hosea is obedient and marries Gomer.

ACT 2: Over time Hosea actually falls in love with Gomer. Think *Pretty Woman* with Richard Gere and Julia Roberts.

ACT 3: Gomer breaks Hosea's heart by going back to her former life and taking up other lovers.

ACT 4: God commands Hosea to pursue, woo, and buy back Gomer.

Many of my favorite movies throughout my life have been the stories of unlikely love.

The high school cheerleader falls in love with the nerdy classmate.

The workaholic CEO ends up marrying the girl in the mailroom. I absolutely love that Hosea genuinely falls in love with Gomer. I have to imagine that these were joyful days for Gomer. She probably never thought she would meet a man who would want her for more than sex. She probably never imagined that a prophet would love and care for her in the way her heart had always longed for.

That's why the first time I read this story I couldn't believe that she would leave her "dream come true" to head back to her old life. Why would you leave the comfort of that love to go back to being used and abused?

Shame becomes an identity that drives us forward into self-abusive actions.

This is the insane way shame works in our lives. Shame blinds us to the miracle of love and forgiveness. My guess is that she felt more comfortable being used and abused than she felt being genuinely loved.

There is a philosophical debate that has gone on for thousands of years. It's summed up in the question, do I love something because it has value, or is it my love that actually gives it value? Is something loved because it's worthy of love or does the very act of loving give it worth? I think it's both.

Shame becomes an identity that drives us forward into self-abusive actions.

There is a love that exists because something is valuable, and there's a love that actually creates value.

Case in point: For the first couple of years of my son Gage's life, he had an inseparable companion. Some kids have a pacifier. Some enjoy a blanket. Still others prefer a blanket. Gage had what we called his "Lovey." It was actually a combination of all three. It was a blanket with an elephant head that he sucked on like a pacifier.

Over time Lovey became mutilated and filthy as Gage carried that thing everywhere he went. You would be shocked at how much our family life revolved around Lovey for several years.

We made trips back to restaurants because Lovey had fallen under the table and we had left without him.

We had late-night search parties looking for Lovey.

We once made a trip back to a hotel where we had left Lovey. And not just five minutes back. We were a good forty-five minutes away.

Lovey even got to go on family vacations, sit at the dinner table, and have full voting rights as a member of the Wilson family.

Looking back, Gage taught all of us an important lesson. There are two kinds of love in this world. A love we express because something brings us value, and a love that can actually create value in something. A love that creates value is a powerful thing. My son loved that raggedy old elephant in such a way that it created value. We still have Lovey stored away for memory's sake. We wouldn't be able to sell that thing at a yard sale for five cents, but you couldn't buy it from me for five hundred dollars.

This is how God loves us. He loves us with a love that creates value. He loves *you* with a love that creates value. And because we have value, we don't need to hold on to our shame.

It's important to note that shame is not produced by past events. Shame is produced by what we believe about those events. Many of us think the past events of our lives have made us undeserving of God's love and forgiveness. Many of us have a hard time accepting God's grace because we tend to only accept the love we think we deserve.

Often our present behavior is directly influenced by what you believe about yourself, and what you believe about yourself is often and unfortunately determined by your past.

Shame stamps us with memories that feed us lies for the rest of our lives. Images of shameful events, moments, and decisions are hard to shake, but what is most crippling is not the memory of the actual events itself but the lie the memory implies telling us how worthless we are.

We have to begin to understand that God does not love us because of our goodness or our faithfulness. He doesn't love us because of our value. He loves us with a love that creates value. His love makes us deserving.

The only shame you carry now is the shame you *choose* to carry.

The chains are gone. You're not a slave to shame. You've been redeemed, set free.

Allowing yourself to be loved by God through the shame and the darkness may be one of the most difficult tasks in the spiritual life. But we need to find ways to allow the grace and love of God to sink in below our levels of guilt and shame.

OUT OF THE PIT

Throughout the book of Isaiah in the Old Testament, the prophet Isaiah points to a great deliverance, which was to come through Jesus. His strong encouragement was to not lose sight of the coming Messiah.

In one section of the book, it appeared as if King Hezekiah was going to die, but Isaiah told the king that God would grant him additional life. He would be healed.

After Hezekiah was healed he wrote, "Lord, by such things people live; and my spirit finds life in them too. You restored me to health and let me live. Surely it was for my benefit that I suffered such anguish. In your love you kept me from the pit of destruction; you have put all my sins behind your back" (Isa. 38:16–17 NIV).

Hezekiah knew well what he deserved. He understood the

grace God was showing him in this moment. He understood God was loving him out of the pit.

Just as God loved Hezekiah out of the pit, he loved your soul out of the pit.

I once heard author and teacher Beth Moore say, "You can't shame someone out of the pit and them stay out of the pit. People are not delivered from their pit because they have been shamed. That shame is what sends us back to the pit over and over and over."

Regardless of what you've been through or done, God wants you.

That's so true, isn't it?

It's shame that led Gomer right back into her being used and abused and being treated like a throwaway object, to go back to what she was comfortable with, which was being used and abused.

It's shame that led Adam and Eve to cover themselves with fig leaves and hide from God.

It's shame that led Will to seek out destructive behaviors in high school and then keep them buried.

Maybe you've gone through divorce, abuse, tragedy, an adulterous relationships, or rape—physical or emotional—and you've been left feeling unwanted and shamed. You've never felt the same since that day. You can't shout over that sort of thing. You can't dig yourself out of that pit. It has the potential to injure something about you that changes how you relate to everyone else for the rest of your life.

No matter how much the shame screams, "You're not wanted," God says, "I want you." Regardless of what you've been through or done, God wants you. He has seen your hurt and has recorded your tears, and he still wants you. He's lifting you out of the pit.

We don't have to go back to the pit, or go back to our self-destructive ways, even though there's a part of us that thinks that's where we belong.

But we don't have to. God loved us right out of that pit, no matter what put us there in the first place. God loves us so much, he wraps himself around us and draws us up.

God does not redeem us based on goodness.

God does not redeem us based on our faithfulness.

He knows the worst about us, but redeems us anyway. We never have to live in the fear that we're not worthy of love.

We are loved with the senseless, seamless, and scandalous love of God. And that changes everything.

3

NO REGRETS

I was lying in bed a few weeks ago, replaying the events in my mind over and over. Earlier in the day I was hunting with a couple of friends. We were having a blast when I got a text from my oldest son, Jett. He was upset because earlier in the week I had promised that he could go hunting with me. As soon as I got his text, I remembered the conversation and he was right: I *had* promised he could go with me. Even though I didn't intentionally set out to mislead and hurt my son, I had. I made a promise and didn't keep it and was instantly filled with regret. Now regret was keeping me awake at night because I knew it was in my power to have kept my promise to my son, but I didn't.

> Regret is harder to bear than other forms of disappointment.

While all pain stings, regret has a unique sting. Regret is not just "I wish things had turned out differently"; it's "I know things could have turned out differently" if I would have acted other than the way I did. Regret is harder to bear than other forms of disappointment.

My family and I are huge Tennessee Titans football fans. We

try to never miss a game and really get into it. My sons and I do chest bumps when the Titans are doing well and lie on the living room floor with our heads in our hands when they're not.

Now when a game is over and we've lost, I might be bummed over the loss but I don't regret the loss, because it wasn't in my power to do anything about it. However, I have several friends who play for the Titans that I've met through our church. I'll usually check in with them after a game, especially if it's been a tough one. And trust me, if it wasn't a good game for them, I'll often hear regret. If I just would have . . . If I'd been a little faster . . . If I'd just made that tackle . . . If I'd just avoided that tackle.

> Time doesn't heal all wounds; God heals wounds.

Most of us look back on some of the decisions we made with varying degrees of regret: I regret dating that guy. I regret losing my temper with my child. I regret quitting that job. I regret not speaking up. So while shame, which we discussed in the previous chapter, is what we often experience because of what someone has done to us, regret is often what we feel for what we've done to others.

And because it's a major theme throughout the Bible, we can find many examples of regret there.

Adam and Eve were filled with regret when they ate the fruit in the garden.

Esau was filled with regret when he sold his birthright for a bowl of stew.

Samson was filled with regret when he told his secret and lost his strength.

Peter was filled with regret when he denied Jesus even though he had sworn that he would not.

Regret is a powerful emotion that often gets more powerful

with the passage of time, which brings us to an important point: time doesn't heal all wounds; God heals wounds.

A MOUNTAIN OF REGRET

One of my favorite people to read about in the Bible is David. I love the brutally honest prayers of this man who is often described as a "man after God's own heart." And yet he made so many poor decisions. He encountered so much pain. He had such a mountain of regret to deal with.

Second Samuel 13–19 describes one of many moments where David dealt with regret. Amnon was David's firstborn son, and he rapes his own half sister, Tamar. Then it says, "he hated her even more than he had loved her" (13:15).

Why did Amnon hate her? Wasn't he the one who just raped her? Wasn't she the victim? There are often two very different reactions to shame and regret.

1. With shame, we are tempted to take the blame for everything.
2. With regret, we are tempted to shift the blame for everything.

If you continuously give into either one of these temptations, it will negatively impact your chances of discovering true hope and health in your life. And while the goal is to put things where they really belong and own what is yours and only what is yours, Amnon obviously shifted the blame. He assassinated Tamar's future and destroyed her integrity and self-esteem.

Amnon didn't even want Tamar afterward. She pleaded with him, "Don't throw me away." She was fighting for the last strands of her being. Amnon called a servant and said, "Throw her out."

The Bible says he hated her with a greater intensity than that with which he had loved her before.

Tamar said, "Raping me was horrible, but not wanting me is worse" (2 Sam. 13:16, paraphrased). When people feel unwanted, it destroys their sense of esteem and value.

Now Amnon was counting on the broken, shame-filled Tamar to keep this whole mess to herself, but she did not go along with his plan. She went on to indicate in a very public way what it was that her brother had done to her.

I believe that Tamar made this bold and courageous move to be honest about this horrible offense because she was confident her father, David, would do the right thing and come to her side. She was banking on **David was paralyzed by his own fallenness.** the fact that as difficult as it might be, her father's character would lead him to intervene and bring some sort of justice to this wrongdoing. She was waiting for her father, who was said to be a man after God's own heart, and who had all the power of the throne behind him to set things right to do something or say something, to stand up for her, to show at least a small measure of the courage.

But as far as we can tell from the text of Scripture, David did nothing. Maybe he was preoccupied with being king. Maybe he was afraid of what Amnon might do in response.

As a dad of three boys, there are times I need to say some really difficult things to my kids and I don't. Sometimes it's because I'm just too tired, but sometimes I'm embarrassed to admit it's because I'm afraid of how my kids might react. Will they love me less? Will they reject me for a period of time? Truth is, I have a deep desire in my heart to matter to my sons.

For David, it might have been something else. I think David was paralyzed by his own fallenness. He had made his fair share of mistakes, most notably murdering Uriah so he could be with Uriah's wife, Bathsheba. David carried a ton of regret around following that series of events and it was impacting him.

It impacted how he led as king, how he loved, and unfortunately for Tamar, how he parented.

I believe his regret and guilt from his own mistakes made him feel he wasn't worthy and so the David who faced Goliath, the David who defied Saul, the David who led a nation, didn't even lift a finger to protect his daughter. His past wasn't his past because it was impacting his present.

David's regret from poor choices in the past was about to lead him into more poor choices in the present.

Some two years passed and one day David's other son Absolom (who was outraged by what his brother Amnon had done to his sister) decided that if his father wasn't going to do anything, he would certainly take matters into his own hands. Absolom decided he would personally avenge the rape of his sister by killing his brother.

After he killed Amnon, Absolom knew that he couldn't stick around. So he ran and went into hiding for three years.

During this three-year period, from what we can tell, David did nothing. He continued to sit idly by while his family was falling apart.

Three years of no contact with his child, his son, who, if David had acted in the first place, might have been set on a totally different path. David did nothing. The text says, "The spirit of King David longed to go forth to Absalom (2 Sam. 13:39 AMP)," but he did not go. He stayed home. He did nothing.

Finally, three years after he had killed his brother, Absalom came back to Jerusalem.

I imagine Absolom wondering, as he walked toward the gate, *What will my dad say? Will he be harsh? Will he forgive?* I remember that feeling of dread all too well whenever I disobeyed my dad as a child. Or now when I see the blue lights flash in my rear-view mirror.

Second Samuel 14:24 tells us that when Absolom came back to Jerusulem, King David said, "He must go to his own house; he must not see my face" (NIV).

Finally, the wondering was over. It was clear: his dad was not going to see him, be with him, or talk with him.

Some more time passed and in desperation Absolom set a field on fire, trying to get his father's attention.

Can you imagine the level of frustration and anger in the heart of a child when the only way they know to get their dad's attention is to set a field on fire? And kids—even when they're grown—will do that. They would like to have their parents' loving attention, but if they can't get it any other way, they'll set fields on fire. Sometimes they'll use drugs or they'll get pregnant or they'll break laws, but they will get their parents' attention one way or another.

NO GOING BACK

Absolom got more and more frustrated, and so over time he built a strong alliance of people. The Bible says that he won over the hearts of the people by being available to them. And so after four years of this, when the moment seemed right, Absalom seized the power of the throne away from his dad and David went into exile.

And I think in the wilderness, David opens his heart again to God. But then David, who was a warrior from his youth, who had led so many campaigns for so many decades, now had to lead one more. Only this time it was against his own son. His troops prepared for battle. He strategized with his generals, and they told him he must stay behind. So he did, but he said to them in chapter 18, "Be gentle with the young man Absalom" (v. 5 NIV).

In other words David was saying, "Do what you got to do, but please make sure my son stays safe. Please don't allow him to be harmed."

Well, if you know the story, you know that during this battle Absolom was killed. And then there was the heart-breaking moment when David found out his son had been killed in the battle: "The king was shaken. He went up to the room over the gateway and wept. As he went, he said: 'Oh my son Absalom! My son, my son Absalom! If only I had died instead of you—O Absalom, my son, my son!'" (v. 33 NIV).

In the wilderness, David opens his heart again to God.

I think a part of why his heart was breaking is because he wondered how this whole sad story might have turned out differently if he would have handled things differently. He had a mountain of regret and wondered, What if?

What if I hadn't followed my lustful desires and slept with Bathsheba who wasn't my wife?

What if I had just turned from my sin instead of trying to make what's not mine, mine, by murdering her husband?

What if I would have sat down with my kids when everything had started to go south and said, Let's talk about our hearts. I want to tell you about my choices, my sorrow. I want to tell you where I went so far wrong, how I messed up. I want to guide you to a better way. Will you forgive me?

But he never had that moment. It was gone forever.

IT'S NOT TOO LATE

Don't let King David's life be just a story you read. There's a little bit of all of us in this story.

Maybe today you're not living with a mountain of regret, but you are starting to create one.

Maybe you're married and there is something going on. There is behavior you're involved in. There is a relationship with somebody. Maybe it's not a full-blown affair yet, but you started crossing little lines.

Maybe God is calling you to take a risk, and you've been shrinking back out of fear, and you're going to get to the end of your life and say, "God, why didn't I trust you? Why did I let fear hold me back from keeping me from not doing the thing that you wanted me to do to serve you?"

> Even if you think it is, it's not too late. You don't have to live with a lifetime of regret.

Maybe you've missed some key moments with your kids and you're just realizing that you've spent years cheating them so you could chase after that corner office.

Maybe there is a hard conversation with somebody that you have been avoiding, and you sense God is telling you, "You get to the end of your life without doing that, there is going to be a pile of regret."

Let's learn from King David's mistakes and not assign ourselves to a lifetime of regret.

If there is a word that needs to be said, say it.

If there is a choice that needs to be made, make it.

If there's something you need to quit, then quit it.

If you can't do it on your own, and you probably can't, get help. And get help soon.

Even if you think it is, it's not too late. You don't have to live with a lifetime of regret.

Know that David's story doesn't exist to make us feel guiltier about our past and faulty decisions. We don't need more guilt.

What we do need is to remember that *when regret is not dealt with directly and receptively, it leads to more regret.* It holds a certain power over us.

But there is hope. And for those of you living with a mountain of regret, it's not too late. As long as you have one more breath, it's not too late.

LETTING GO

I'll be honest. I have a hard time letting go of things. My closet is the best example of this. I have shirts hanging in my closet that I haven't worn in over five years. I have shoes stacked on the floor of my closet that I bet I haven't worn in close to a decade. I have no idea why I hold on to these things.

The other day my wife, Brandi, secretly went through my closet and had formed a massive pile of things that she was going to take to the Goodwill. When she wasn't watching, I went through the pile and removed several of the items, which I promptly returned to my closet.

Because most of us have such a difficult time letting go, clutter is a growing problem in our culture—whether in our homes, purses, briefcases, or offices.

But I believe there's an "inner clutter," which is a much more severe problem in my life and probably in yours.

While my mess of a closet isn't really hurting anyone, my "inner clutter" is impacting everything about me and everyone around me.

We have a tendency to hang on tightly to outdated thoughts and disturbing memories, or we cling to sentimental parts of our past we feel are too meaningful to abandon. Maybe you've had this happen. You're driving along listening to the car radio when a certain song comes on that instantly takes you back to a time when you were crushed, heartbroken, or devastated. Suddenly, all those painful emotions come flooding in once again. When that happens, we always have the choice of turning the dial, but we usually go on listening and hurting. Something seems to always be drawing us back into the past.

There is an ancient Egyptian proverb that says, "The marksman hitteth the target partly by pulling, partly by letting go. The boatsman reacheth the landing partly by pulling, partly by letting go."

It's much the same with our lives. We can get a good start by pulling from the past with all its disappointments, regrets, and heartache, but after we've learned from the past, there has to be a release or a letting go of that past.

> The cross is the only safe place for human regret.

How often do we clutch the burdens of our own guilt and regrets in our life, when we have the option of releasing them? There are many things we need to release in order to experience true freedom.

Condemning inner voices whisper to us that we should have spent more time with our spouse or children; been a better wife, mom, daughter, or friend; taken a job to contribute to the family income (or stayed home with the children while they were small—moms just can't win!); accepted the promotion; turned down the offer; said no to temptation. The list of our inner voices is endless!

We tell ourselves we could have tried harder, been more discerning, tuned into another's needs, kept our cool, stayed calm, not fought back, learned better ways to handle a difficult situation, stayed away, kept our mouth shut, saved up instead of going into debt, or prayed more.

Then we begin to live in the fantasy world of if only. If only

I had listened to my parents, if only I had finished my degree, if only I hadn't married so young, and the list goes on.

This is a waste of effort, time, and energy, because we can't go back and change those things.

The cross is the only safe place for human regret.

Because of the cross, we don't have to minimize our regret or deny our regret. We bring all of our regrets to the foot of the cross. We release them because our God is in the redemption business, and at the foot of the cross, regret can turn into repentance, and repentance can turn into redemption.

If you're in the process of creating a mountain of regret, stop! If you're carrying a weight of regret on your back that you can't fix, it's in the past—put it down and clean it out, because it's time to make room for something new.

CHOICE TWO:

CHOOSING TO BE OKAY WITH NOT BEING OKAY

4

I CAN'T (CONFESSION)

A couple weeks ago I was in the house when I heard one of my boys screaming at the top of his lungs in the backyard. "Daddy, come here! Daddy, come here!" My first thought was, *He better be bleeding as loud as he's screaming.*

As I ran out of the house, Gage called, "Dad, you have to see this."

I kept asking, "What is it? What is it?" I couldn't figure out what he was looking at, but he just said to come and look.

When I finally reached him, I saw it—a five-foot-long black snake curled up just a couple feet away. I let out a scream so loud, it made his earlier screaming sound like a whisper. If there's one thing that terrifies me, it's snakes. I don't care if it's a harmless black snake. They still freak me out.

We spent hours that day trying to get that snake out of our backyard. Hundreds of screams, a hoe, and a rake later, we actually coerced it to go under the fence and leave our backyard.

I think fear is an inescapable reality of life. But while fearing something is one thing, allowing it to paralyze us and keep us from moving forward is another. As trivial as my fear of snakes sounds, if we didn't keep trying to make it leave our backyard, I'd still be afraid to step outside.

Anything God leads us to do will initially involve some level of fear. And this is where many of us walk away.

The poet Ralph Waldo Emerson once said, "Fear defeats more people than any other one thing in the world."[1]

Anything God leads us to do will initially involve some level of fear.

Fear will lead to mediocrity. It leads to *should haves* and *could haves*, and excuses like "I'm too old" or "I'm too young."

But the reality is, while fear can taunt you, it can't touch you.

It can attempt to lead you, but you don't have to follow.

It will always try to rule, but there is a power within you that can defeat it.

YOUR GREATEST FEAR

There are a lot of things in this life to fear: snakes, tight spaces, heights, the doctor, the dark, just to name a few.

But I think one of our greatest fears is the fear of being found out.

It's why we spend so much time posturing and pretending to be someone we're not. We spend so much time trying to cover the mistakes of our past that we truly don't even know who we are anymore.

You know what's interesting about this fear? It's very closely tied to one of our greatest desires. While we fear being found out, we simultaneously long to be fully known and fully loved.

But here's the problem: you can only be loved to the extent that you are known.

Let me explain. If my wife, Brandi, looks me in the eyes and tells me she loves me, my heart can't fully accept her love if I'm hiding things from her.

It wants to, but it can't. Even though I hear those words, my heart rejects a portion of it because in my mind I'm thinking, *If she knew what I did last week ... or last year ... she wouldn't say that. If she knew the real me, there's no way she would love me like she says she loves me.*

This is why you can only be loved to the extent that you are known.

Years ago I heard Pastor Andy Stanley say, "The reason we fear the consequences of confession is because we've yet to realize the consequences of concealment."

And the consequence of concealment is that you go your whole life with your past not being your past. You go your whole life allowing regret and guilt to devour you. You go your whole life never feeling like you're completely known or loved by anyone.

WASTING AWAY

Many of the Psalms are attributed to David, who we talked about in the last chapter. We took a peak into a very difficult season of David's life where his lack of action led to a mountain of regret.

As I shared earlier, I believe he was paralyzed by the guilt of his past. However, somewhere along his journey he discovered the freedom that comes along with confession.

He wrote about this journey from confession to forgiveness in Psalm 32.

> Oh, what joy for those
> whose rebellion is forgiven,
> whose sin is put out of sight!
> Yes, what joy for those
> whose record the LORD has cleared
> of sin,
> whose lives are lived in complete
> honesty! (vv. 1–2)

But why do we need to confess sin in the first place? David begins by saying confession is for our sake. Sometimes we think confession is for God's sake, like our sins sort of annoy him and some act of confession will appease him. But David says, "No! Confession is for you." There's a blessing in this for you. There's something God wants to give to you. This is about your quality of life.

Notice all the other blessings David just sort of skips over. He doesn't talk about the blessing of wealth, or of power, or of reputation, all the things we would pursue. David is saying, "No! Those things can't heal us." We chase after them like they could, but they can't heal us. David is saying, "The way to find blessing is by being forgiven."

Because David understands that our most fundamental problem is actually a spiritual one.

He continues in Psalm 32:

> *When I refused to confess my sin,*
> *I was weak and miserable,*
> *and I groaned all day long.*
> *Day and night your hand of discipline*
> *was heavy on me.*
> *My strength evaporated like water*
> *in the summer heat. (vv. 3–4)*

In essence, David is saying, *When I kept silent, when I was hiding, when I wasn't talking about it, when I was keeping it secret, I felt like I was dying inside.*

I imagine most of us can relate to this feeling in some way or another, because there are a lot of things in our lives we keep silent about. Things we feel ashamed of: family problems, compulsive habits, sexual addiction, to name a few. While silence in the moment might seem like the best, safest way to handle it, silence always leads to more pain and guilt and festering inside. It corrodes away our soul. It corrodes away our spirit. And it always, always, always begins to affect other parts of our lives.

> Silence always leads to more pain and guilt and festering inside.

It's amazing how many of us are just stuck in the religious routine. We sing songs, serve in ministries, attend Bible studies, throw money into the offering plate. Week in and week out, we go through the same routine and nobody knows we're dying inside. Nobody knows we have these secret sins that are keeping us from moving forward. No one knows about it.

No one knows about it—but *you* know about it. God knows about it.

We continue looking at Psalm 32 to see how David was finally able to let go of his guilt.

Finally, I confessed all my sins to you
and stopped trying to hide them.
I said to myself, "I will confess my
rebellion to the LORD."
And you forgave me! All my guilt is
gone. (v. 5)

It almost seems too easy, doesn't it? But there's no process or ritual to go through, no promising anything or having to do something. *In fact, confession isn't doing something about our sin; rather, it means admitting that we can't do anything about our sin.*

There is something intrinsically broken and sinful in every human being. Merely human efforts (education, environment, therapy) cannot cure the sin problem. My brokenness, like yours, is very complex. Jesus comes as the Great Physician. He comes for sick people who wrestle with sin, not for people who pretend they're healthy.

If we want to heal, we need to be honest with God and ourselves and each other. Some of you are carrying around secrets that are killing you. Maybe it's about your past, sexuality, impulses, bitterness, anger, finances, marriage, work, or whatever. But if you keep playing the game and keeping silent about your secrets, you can't heal and move forward.

> If we want to heal, we need to be honest with God and ourselves and each other.

As David said in the Psalms, until he dealt with the problem of guilt and sin in his life, all this other stuff he was doing—including being the king of Israel—was really quite pointless. He was going about his life, and he was going about his duties, but his bones were wasting away. He was groaning all day long. He felt like God's hand was heavy upon him, that his strength was sapped. He needed to come clean.

I'M NOT OKAY

I met a friend for coffee earlier this week to just catch up. It had been several months since we had spent any significant time with each other. We sat down with our coffee and I started by, almost out of habit, just asking, "How are you, man?" He shot back with the typical "I'm good. Life is busy, but I'm good."

There was something inside of me that said I needed to push back a bit, so I did something I don't normally do. I responded by saying, "Let me rephrase my question: How are you *really* doing?"

There was an uncomfortably long pause. He looked out the window of the coffee shop, and I could tell he was starting to tear up. I nervously started to fidget and asked, "You okay?"

He finally looked back at me and said, "No. I'm not okay."

For the next hour we would have one of the most real, authentic conversations about fears, marriage, and God's purpose. He had the chance to share some things that had really been holding him in bondage. And to think we almost missed this conversation.

Somewhere along the way I think as Christians we picked up this idea that somehow Christians should be "beyond" or "above" being hurt. We think if we were stronger or better Christians that we wouldn't hurt so much.

All the while you keep telling yourself this same thing over and over . . .

Nothing is really wrong with me.

Nothing is really wrong with me.

Nothing is really wrong with me.

You say it over and over until you actually start to believe it.

First, we deceive ourselves, and then we convince others that we are not deceiving ourselves. Deception typically flows in two directions: inward as we try to convince ourselves, and then outward as we try to convince others.

Sin thrives on self-deception, and self-deception thrives on silence. Before we can specifically confess sin, we have to admit we're broken, shattered, hurting, not okay or fine. As long as we're deceiving ourselves and pretending to have it all together, we won't see the need for confession.

Which is why we have to start by confessing to God that . . .

We're not okay.

We're not fine.

My past hurts are causing me to act out in a way that is not pleasing to God and is destroying the person he created me to be.

The apostle James wrote in the New Testament, "Confess your sins one to each other and pray for each other so that you may be healed" (James 5:16 NIV).

So while there is a healing power in confession to God, there's also a certain healing that takes place when we confess to each other.

I heard a pastor once talk about a service they held where the theme was confession. At the end of the service they invited individuals and families to come forward and literally attach their sins to a cross they had erected at the front of the church as a symbol of Christ's forgiveness through the cross.

One family came forward together and wrote down their confessions anonymously, folded up their papers, and pinned them to the cross like everyone else was doing. The youngest of the family, a six-year-old, wrote, "God, I'm sorry because I lie."

Then he signed his name. He didn't fold it up. He pinned it right there to the front of the cross.

Pride can often be found behind other sin.

His parents asked him, "Why did you put your name on it? Don't you want to fold it up so no one can see?"

The boy answered, "I wrote my name on it because I want everyone to see because if they know it was me, maybe they can help me stop."

This little six-year-old was on to something.

There is breakthrough that happens when we confess to other people. There is a chain that is broken.

Pride can often be found behind other sin. So in confession to another person, there is a profound humiliation that accompanies. We're admitting we don't have it all together. We're not okay. We need help.

And a beautiful thing often happens when we confess to another person. It's called community.

Our past sins and pain long to live in hiddenness. They almost always drag us away from community because the more lonely we are, the more destructive and powerful our past becomes.

I love the way the German theologian Dietrich Bonhoeffer put it in his book *Life Together*:

> In confession there occurs a breakthrough to the cross. The root of all sin is pride, superbia. I want to be for myself; I have a right to be myself, a right to my hatred and my desires, my life and my death. The spirit and flesh of human beings are inflamed by pride, for it is precisely in their wickedness that human beings want to be like God. Confession in the presence of another believer is the most profound kind of humiliation. It hurts, makes one feel small; it deals a terrible blow to one's pride. To stand there before another Christian as a sinner is an almost unbearable disgrace. By confessing actual sins the old self dies a painful, humiliating death before the eyes of another Christian. Because this humiliation is so difficult, we keep thinking we can avoid confessing to one another. Our eyes are so blinded that they no longer see the promise and the glory of such humiliation.[2]

I think this is why Jesus clearly desires for us to do community in a different way.

In the gospel of Matthew, a very concerned Jesus spoke to the human tendency to hide, pretend, and posture: "What sorrow awaits you teachers of religious law and you Pharisees. Hypocrites! For you are like whitewashed tombs—beautiful on the outside but filled on the inside with dead people's bones and all sorts of impurity. Outwardly you look like righteous people, but inwardly your hearts are filled with hypocrisy and lawlessness" (23:27–28).

Jesus says, in this community, called the church, we're going to do things differently: we will honor the costly humiliating confession of brokenness and sin more than the appearance of invulnerability and impressiveness.

In his book *Addiction and Virtue*, Kent Dunnington shared

that one of the primary discoveries of twelve-step communities is that utterly honest, open relationships of humiliating vulnerability are central to healing.

Confession in the presence of another believer is the most profound kind of humiliation.

Have you ever been to an AA group or something similar? One of the first things you'll notice will be people standing up and introducing themselves like, "My name is John. I'm an alcoholic. I'm an addict. I'm a drunk." It's a huge moment and everyone in the circle recognizes this is a huge step in a spiritual battle.

There are all kinds of forces of darkness trying to keep that person from coming into the light and making that statement. Everybody knows they fight the same battle. So when that confession gets made in that little twelve-step group in that basement, or health club or church or wherever it is, everybody celebrates the confession.

Unfortunately in the church today, this kind of honesty, confession, and community has become totally optional. It's unfortunate because I think Jesus made it clear that in his community such things wouldn't be optional. There's no other way to find healing from our past.

SET FREE

Now we can't miss that David ends this prayer of confession not with despair, not with discouragement, not with depression, not with self-doubt. He ends with joy.

For you are my hiding place;
you protect me from trouble.
You surround me with songs of
victory. (Ps. 32:7)

This is a song of victory because he's been forgiven. He has been set free.

You've been forgiven. You have been set free.

Your lying schemes, forgiven.

Your lustful acts, forgiven.

Your self-seeking manipulation, forgiven.

Your religious hypocrisy, forgiven.

All the guilt, all the shame, all the stuff you've been carrying maybe for years and years and years . . . you can be set free.

God has come in the person of Jesus to set you free. There is no story in the world like the story of redemption, and it can be your story.

Let the story of you be a story of redemption.

5

THE HEALER

Several years ago Brandi and I met this great couple who had a daughter who played on the basketball team with our son. We knew from the get-go that Ty and Lori would be the kind of people we would want to do life with. Ty was at one time training to be an Olympic track-and-field athlete and the obvious life of the party. Lori was a bit more reserved but laughed at all of my jokes, which gained her instant access to my inner circle.

Our kids ended up playing multiple sports together, so we spent Saturdays and some weeknights hanging out at the park and just chatting. We'd often go out to eat afterward and talk about everything from our marriages to parenting to our favorite TV shows.

One of the refreshing things about our relationship with them was that it didn't involve our church. They knew what I did for a living, but they had never seen our church or attended our church, so they really didn't even know how to talk or ask about it, which was fine with me. We did, however, talk about Jesus from time to time. I loved the simple innocence they had for Jesus and his love and wondering why all people didn't live and love like him.

One night on the way home after dinner I asked Brandi, "Do

you see how Ty lights up anytime I talk about second chances or grace or anything like that? It's like something goes off in his mind and he energetically dives into the conversation." She replied, "I have noticed that. I wonder what's that about?"

About a year into our friendship with them, Brandi was working out with a friend of hers. This innocent, workout session quickly took a sharp turn when her friend asked, "Brandi, aren't you and Pete friends with Ty and Lori?"

Brandi said, "Sure, we are. We met them through our kids' sports teams and now we hang out with them quite a bit."

Her friend quickly followed up with, "Brandi, do you know about Ty?"

"What about Ty?" she asked.

There was a long pause and then the woman with a very plastic sense of compassion said, "Ty is a sex offender. When he was still training at a high level, he was also coaching some high school students and was accused of having sexual relations with an underage girl."

Later that night Brandi told me that she heard nothing else for the rest of the workout session. She was shocked and couldn't believe it.

That evening Brandi and I sat in front of the computer looking up old news articles. It seems as if much of what the women had said was true. At age twenty-two (a little over twenty years ago), Ty had, in fact, had a sexual relationship with a seventeen-year-old senior at the school where he was a coach. The family pressed charges and for the rest of his life Ty would be known as a "sex offender."

As a sex offender there are many rules that he must abide by. These laws assume once a sex offender, always a sex offender. Now we could argue if all of these safeguards are necessary, but the bottom line is that such laws exist to protect the victims whose lives have been shattered by such a sexual offense.

Community corrections officers must approve sex offenders' residential choices and living arrangements, and they cannot move without permission. Sex offenders often cannot own or control personal computers and must allow their community corrections officers to inspect every part of their homes. Many offenders must obtain psycho-sexual evaluations and treatment from state-certified sexual deviancy counselors. Offenders cannot purchase, possess, or consume any mind- or mood-altering substances, including alcohol or drugs that have not been prescribed by doctors. They may have to undergo chemical dependency treatment and follow prescribed treatment, which may include Alcoholics Anonymous or other recovery meetings. Offenders must disclose information about their conviction(s) to potential adult sexual partners before beginning sexual relationships. They also must inform their CCO of romantic relationships so they can ensure no potential child victims are accessible. Some offenders may be required by their CCO to disclose their criminal history to their families and friends. Contact with minors is monitored and managed.

Ty was not allowed to be on school property, even to pick up his own children, without first checking in with the principal, to whom he would have to disclose that he was in fact a "sex offender." Ty loved athletics, but he would never be allowed to coach a sports team for one of his kids.

Every time they moved, Ty had to register their new address with law enforcement. The address changes of sex offenders is usually printed in the paper and on certain websites, so it wasn't uncommon for them to find signs in the front yard of their new home that said things like "Dirty Perverts Not Wanted Here," "Go to Hell but Not Our Neighborhood," "Shame on You," and "Child Molester Lives Here."

Despite pressure from many in the community, Brandi and I

haven't changed our relationship with Ty and Lori. We've asked more questions, we've talked about the ramifications of it, but we felt that if they ever needed close friends now would be the time.

This past year has been brutal for Ty. He's finally come to the realization that his inexcusable sin will haunt him until his dying breath, but he's not bitter about it. He knows he deserves punishment, but it kills him to see his wife and children impacted so deeply.

Just a few months ago, there was a brief light of hope as they were so thrilled to get their daughter into one of the best private schools in the South. She had tried out for their volleyball team and was so excited about playing for them this year. Two weeks into the school year, someone on the administration was sent an anonymous letter detailing Ty's past. Within two days their daughter was dismissed from the school. Ty's daughter was wrecked and this was a new low for Ty as well.

A few weeks later Ty found out his mother had inoperable colon cancer. His mother, who had stood by his side through years of bad mistakes and public ridicule. His mother, who he knew he had severely disappointed in so many ways through the years. His mother, who had loved him unconditionally through it all, only had months to live.

BANISHED

There's only one condition or sin I can think of during Jesus' time that was treated like such social outcasts as sex offenders are today, and that would be leprosy. In both cases the laws were set up not so much to embarrass the offender, but to keep the rest of society safe.

There was a man living with leprosy during the time of Jesus. We can imagine that one day he was plowing in the field and he noticed a little white spot on his hand. Concerned but not overly alarmed that night at dinner, he showed his wife the spot. She gently told him they should probably keep an eye on it. By this point there were actually several white spots and his kids teased him about what it might be.

Over the next couple of days the spots continued to multiply and now these white spots became nodules, which began to ooze fluid. Now his wife was concerned, and she begged him to go see the priest. The priest in these days was also like the local health official.

As the law required, the priest told him he would have to be quarantined for fourteen days. Two weeks of waiting and wondering what it might be. I'm sure there were times he wondered if it could be the dreaded leprosy, but I bet he was begging God, any God, to heal him.

At the end of the two weeks, the priest broke the bad news: "You have leprosy and are going to die. You must be banished, separated away with others like yourself."

"Wait, I have to tell my wife good-bye."

"No, that's not possible. You can never go near her or your family again."

"Wait, just one hug from my little girl!"

"No, you cannot. Never again can you touch a clean person. You are contagious."

That day he was sent off to a leper colony to die. From then on if he by some small chance saw anyone who was not a part of the colony, he would have to yell out, "Unclean, unclean."

I imagine he watched his children grow up from a distance. They approached from the safety of a few hundred feet and would wave at him, leaving him food and messages. Perhaps he received a note from his daughter that simply said, "Daddy, we love you and miss you. I want to give you a hug more than anything in the world. I'm being a good girl. I promise. Please don't forget me."

Soon the sores covered his whole body, became ulcerated, and began to bleed. Then the flesh started falling off of his body, sometimes in large portions—fingers and toes first, perhaps an ear or part of the nose. Now even his only family couldn't stand to see him. It was too much, so the distant visits, the meals, the notes started to be fewer and further between.

At night when he tried to sleep, the rats came to eat off of his flesh. His voice became raspy and his breath wheezy, and then he knew there wasn't much longer for him. Death was inevitable.

TOUCHING THE UNTOUCHABLE

There are more healings of lepers than any other kind of story in the four Gospels. Jesus healed a lot of lepers. Apparently, *leprosy* in the New Testament is kind of a generic word. According to author Richard Rohr, "'Lepers' were people who, for some reason, were told they were physically unacceptable. They were people who were considered taboo, contagious, disabled, dangerous, or excluded for all kinds of reasons." Even though we understand today that leprosy is a physical condition, it was associated with sin and considered both a physical *and* a spiritual disease in Bible times.

Back to our story: One day this man with leprosy did something unexpected, something no other leper would do.

Maybe it was out of desperation.

Maybe he couldn't stand the idea of not seeing his family again.

Maybe he had tremendous faith or thought he had nothing left to lose.

But regardless the reason, one day he left the leper colony where he was living exiled from society to find this man named Jesus who he had heard was doing amazing miracles.

The gospel of Luke records this unforeseen moment: "While Jesus was in one of the towns, a man came along who was covered with leprosy. When he saw Jesus, he fell with his face to the ground and begged him, 'Lord, if you are willing, you can make me clean'" (Luke 5:12 NIV).

As he approached Jesus that day, he would have had to proclaim, "Unclean, unclean!" If there was anyone around, we can assume they all scattered away to a safe distance.

It was against the law for a person who had leprosy to touch anybody who was not leprous. Any rabbi, like Jesus, knew this. Leprosy is the one disease in which a person was not just sick but also unclean. So this man didn't have to just be healed; he had to be cleansed.

But there was something about this Rabbi Jesus that inspired this leper to violate the law and approach him. Suffering people are drawn to Jesus throughout the New Testament because he was known to be a compassionate healer.

Look at how Jesus responds to this man: "Jesus reached out his hand and touched the man. 'I am willing,' he said. 'Be clean!' And immediately the leprosy left him" (v. 13 NIV).

And Jesus does something wonderful. You would expect if a rabbi was able to heal, that he would heal the guy first and then touch him, right? This only makes sense. But Jesus doesn't do that. The text deliberately tells us Jesus touches him while he still has leprosy and then says, "Be clean." Be healed.

With his touch, Jesus not only heals this man of his disease but reintroduces him to community. He makes him socially acceptable again.

Suffering people so often are starved to be touched. When somebody loves us, when they put their arms around us, when they give us a hug, it's literally life-giving.

Being in ministry, I've had the privilege to partner with many different nonprofits and organizations that reach out to those who may be suffering. This past summer I traveled with Pastor Rick Warren and his wife, Kay, to Washington, D.C., to attend the International AIDS Conference in order to learn how we can better serve and love on people infected with this virus. We've come a long way in how we react and treat HIV/AIDS here in the United States over the past twenty years, but there are still so many preconceived notions that exist. I spent the majority of my time over those five days just listening to and loving on people with AIDS. I bet I hugged thousands of people with AIDS that week.

> Jesus longs to touch the parts of your heart that you are withholding from him.

I've also been the recipient of—and experienced the power of—a hug. And I hope you have as well. There's nothing else like it. There's power in a hug. In a simple touch.

Jesus wants this leper to remember this touch, so he does what nobody else would do: Jesus touches the untouchable. The last thing that happens to this guy before he's healed is that he's touched in his uncleanness.

Is there a part of you that you think is untouchable? Maybe there's something that happened in your past that is so off-limits because you think it's unredeemable. Jesus longs to touch the parts of your heart that you are withholding from him because those are the parts that need the most healing.

A pastor I've been friends with for over a decade recently came clean with me about his past prescription drug problem, which ruled his life for almost twenty years. He took an oxycontin pill every Sunday morning for years, as he felt it helped him deal with the stress of Sunday mornings. He actually thought it made him a better pastor. It eventually turned into him taking them daily to cope, and it almost ruined his marriage and his church.

He said, "Pete, I gave God *almost* everything. I gave him my vocation, my money, my heart in worship, my family; I gave him everything but this area of my heart diseased with this prescription addiction. And that disease gripped my heart. And I thought it was God's problem, that he wasn't strong enough or faithful enough to answer my prayer. But I learned that the disease of our heart loses its power when we acknowledge it, confess it to God, and share it with someone we trust." As embarrassing as it was, he eventually confessed to his elders who then walked him through getting help. He has confessed his sin, has found healing from God, and is still in ministry today.

Our leprosy can be an addiction or shame or anything else we're trying to hide. I'm learning daily that Jesus is willing; in fact, he's longing to heal and make us free.

A HEALING GOD

If you ever doubt the heart of our great God, just read through the Gospels and look at the life of Jesus. He proves there is a good God who cares about brokenness: spiritual brokenness, physical brokenness, and emotional brokenness. Jesus wants to heal. And he doesn't only want to heal the shame that has been brought upon you because of someone else's actions. He also wants to heal the shame that you carry that is a direct result of something you've done.

When Jesus encountered the sick woman in Luke 13, he called out to her. There may have been many fine people present that day, but Jesus didn't call them forward. He reached around all of them and found that crippled woman in the back. He called forth the wounded, hurting person with a past.

The feeble, sickly woman must have thought, *He wants me. He wants me. I'm frayed and torn, but he wants me. I have been through trouble. I have been through this trauma, but he wants me.*

Perhaps she thought no one would ever want her again, but Jesus wanted her. She was disabled and probably filled with insecurities. Yet Jesus still chose to heal her.

Another time Jesus asked a blind man,

"What do you want me to do for you?"

"Lord, I want to see," [the blind man] replied.

Jesus said to him, "Receive your sight; your faith has healed you." Immediately [the man] received his sight and followed Jesus, praising God. When all the people saw it, they also praised God. (Luke 18:41–43 NIV)

Right now I'm praying that you understand this deeply: God sees you struggling, and he knows all about your pain. He knows what happened to you eighteen years ago or ten years ago or even last week. With patience he waits for you. As the father waited for the prodigal son, Jesus says to the hurting and crippled, "I want you enough to wait for you to hobble your way back home."

Jesus says, I'm going to renew you and release you. I'm going to tell you who you really are.

A woman who has been bleeding for over a decade fights through a crowd to touch his robes (see Luke 8:43–48).

A blind man named Bartimaeus shouts so loudly to Jesus in his desperation that the crowd tells him to shut up. But he will not be quiet: "Jesus, Son of David, have mercy on me!" (see Mark 10:46–52).

A Roman centurion with a servant who is suffering at home crosses all kinds of ethnic barriers to come before Jesus and ask, "Would you have mercy on my servant? You don't even have to come to my home. For I'm a man with authority, and I live under authority, and I know how it works. Jesus, just say the word" (see Luke 7:2–10).

Jesus came to proclaim the kingdom of God, and that meant healing—healing for people's bodies and healing for people's souls.

One time some friends broke through the roof of a house of somebody to get their paralyzed buddy to Jesus. And when Jesus looked at this man, his first words were, "Your sins are forgiven." And people got mad about this. And Jesus said, "What's harder? To forgive sin or to heal a body?" He continued. "So that you may understand the Son of Man has now been given all authority," he also heals the guy's body. He heals bodies. He heals souls (see Luke 5:17–26).

Healing was central to Jesus' mission but was not just something he did to attract big crowds; it was a sign that, in Jesus, God's work to heal human brokenness has begun.

HELP ME

"Jesus, help me" is one of the most honorable things a person can say. Someone who has something doesn't ask for help. The spiritually destitute person has nothing to offer, and that is exactly what God requires of us.

Nothing.

We have nothing we can offer God. All our good deeds and works mean nothing.

Last week my friend Ty's mom, who I told you about earlier in the chapter, died from colon cancer. Ty was devastated as you might imagine. His lifelong cheerleader who stood by his side when nobody else would was gone.

As a pastor, I do quite a few funerals. An interesting trend I've seen over the past few years is that more and more people seem to be planning out their own funerals. They'll leave notes detailing a poem, or song, or maybe a scripture they would like to incorporate.

Let the story of you be a story of forgiveness and redemption.

As he was leaving the funeral home from which his family had been making the funeral arrangements, Ty called me. "My mom planned out much of her funeral, and she wanted me to read something. You're going to get a kick out of this, Pete, because she left behind a couple verses that she wants me to stand up and read."

I responded, "That's great, Ty. I know that will mean a lot to her—and to you as well."

There was a long pause before he replied. "Um, Pete, I don't really understand what this verse she left for me means, but I got a feeling there's a message or something she wanted me to get."

"Tell me what it is, and I'll look it up for you."

"Lamentations 3:21–23."

I quickly looked it up and read it out loud on the phone to him. "'Yet I still dare to hope when I remember this: The faithful love of the Lord never ends! His mercies never cease. Great is his faithfulness; his mercies begin afresh each morning.'" I said, "Ty, man, I love this verse. Do you know what your mom is trying to say to you? She wants you to know that your sin doesn't make you second-class. She wants you to experience the healing power of Jesus' forgiveness, which is available to us fresh each morning. She wants you to know that regardless of what you've done or where you've been that Jesus is here to set you free."

I couldn't help but think the rest of the day how powerful of a move that was for a dying mom to want to bestow on her struggling son. While the entire world looked at Ty and thought "sexual offender," his mom looked at him and thought "forgiven."

God has come in the person of Jesus to set you free. On the cross, the Son of God was stripped naked, and his arms were stretched out, publicly humiliating him and literally exposing him for the world to see. He was exposed to all of our sins so they could be covered. The cross is the greatest act of forgiveness in the history of humanity, and it can be your forgiveness. This freedom can be your freedom. This redemption can be your redemption.

God is faithfully healing our brokenness.

He is restoring hope and freedom.

Let the story of you be a story of forgiveness and redemption.

Let hope in.

6

EMBRACING THE PAST

This week I had the opportunity to sit down with Scott Hamilton, who is a former gold medalist in figure skating. Scott was my generation's Michael Phelps. Starting in 1981 he won seventeen National or World Figure Skating Titles in a row.

After competing in the Olympics, Scott turned professional and spent years touring with the Ice Capades and Stars on Ice.

Throughout those years, his fans surely would have thought he was on top of the world. Surely he was happy and successful. The truth is, as Scott put it, there was a huge part of his life that he didn't enjoy at all. It seemed like one tragic thing after another. Friendships had disappeared, relationships had failed, and he felt guilty.

Through a series of events Scott grew in his faith in Christ and eventually got to a place where he started to believe his "curses" were actually blessings. This outlook served him well because he eventually had to fight testicular cancer and two brain tumors.

When he was first diagnosed with cancer, Scott was overcome with fear and embarrassment. He was afraid because he had watched his mother die of cancer. He was embarrassed because he didn't want people to know he had testicular cancer.

"But I quickly learned, and even embraced, what many survivors call the 'gift' of cancer," Scott said. He didn't choose his childhood where he spent years fighting a mystery illness. He didn't choose his birth mom putting him up for adoption. He didn't choose whether his own cancer or the brain tumor would come back.

But Scott did choose hope. And he learned that there's a responsibility that comes along with letting hope in. Once you let hope in, you have a responsibility—and often a desire—to then let that hope out.

Scott now spends a great deal of his time traveling the world raising money and awareness for cancer research. He speaks frequently, helping groups that are searching for hope understand that it's how you look at your past suffering, how you deal with it, that will define you.

> Most of us have at least some fragment of yesterday in our hearts, and there's no doubt that it has shaped who we are.

On more than one occasion Scott has admitted that his past struggles are an odd blessing, one that he would never choose, yet it is a powerful force that enhances his life. As he puts it, "Any challenge—be it romantic, physical, job-related, athletic, mental, financial—can also serve as a gift if we allow it to."

Most of us have at least some fragment of yesterday in our hearts, and there's no doubt that it has shaped who we are. We have been changed by it. We would not be who we are today had we not fallen and stumbled, been hurt or abused.

We really don't have a choice on whether the past has impacted us. But we do, however, get to choose if we embrace it. We get to choose if our past with all of its unique sorrows and joys helps us grow, if we learn from it, or if we use it to bless others.

I've struggled with something for a while, and at times it makes me wonder if my faith is just too small or if I don't have a good understanding of God's healing power. I struggle with wondering if our hurt, damaged, weak areas caused by the injury of our past ever really becomes "whole."

Don't shut the book just yet. While I do believe and have no doubt that Christ transforms lives, I question if our lives ever become "whole" or if it's God's grace that makes up the difference. Are we fully healed from our past, or do we just learn to lean on Christ in those areas, which leads to letting hope in?

I'm finally accepting my brokenness. And by "accepting it," I don't mean I've given up on transformation. Looking back, I'm realizing I had never fully come to terms with my brokenness.

I pretended like my parents' divorce never impacted me.

I tried to cover up the hurt caused by a miscarriage Brandi and I had.

I attempted to ignore how the betrayal of some close friends had damaged me.

Oh, I knew I was broken, I knew I was a sinner, and I knew I continually disappointed God. I just couldn't accept that part of me. It was a part of me that embarrassed me. It was part of me that I wanted to hide from everyone else, including God. I continually felt the need to apologize, to run from my weaknesses, to deny who I was and concentrate on what I should be. I was broken, yes, but I was continually trying never to be broken again.

But all of this was motivated from this desire to "please God." I needed to learn to "trust" him instead. The book of 2 Timothy says that, "if we are faithless, he remains faithful" (2:13 NIV).

There are very few people who I trust completely. Even the really "good" people in my life who have given me no reason to doubt them can only be trusted at about a 90 percent level. I know this and so do many of you. We have a hard time trusting people because so many of them have broken promises to us.

And the reality is, we've broken quite a few promises along the journey, so we know the human tendencies well.

Some of you were physically, emotionally, or maybe even sexually abused growing up. The very people who were supposed to be there to protect you, abused you. How can you trust after that? You've been lied to your whole life.

Your parents made a promise to each other that they would love each other until death. But instead they split when things got tough.

Your boss promised to take care of you, but when you stopped producing in the way he wanted, not only did he not protect you but he fired you.

Our lives are full of broken promises and so we start to doubt everyone, and that eventually spills over to our relationship with God. But we have to remember that God is "other." He is not like us. He is faithful even when we're faithless. We can trust him.

Especially in our brokenness.

BEYOND WHAT YOU CAN HANDLE

There was one particular phrase that I seemed to hear over and over growing up in the church. It was the phrase "God will never give you more than you can handle."

It sounds so sweet and biblical and like something my grandmother would have crocheted and hung on the wall in her house. The problem is nothing could be further from the truth. I'm not sure where we got such wacked theology, but here's the truth: Throughout life we will face one situation after another that will be completely beyond what we can handle.

In fact, in a letter to the Corinthians, the apostle Paul said, "But he said to me, 'My grace is sufficient for you, for my power is made perfect in weakness.' That is why, for Christ's sake, I delight in weaknesses, in insults, in hardships, in persecutions, in difficulties. For when I am weak, then I am strong" (2 Cor. 12:9–10 NIV).

When we admit our weakness, we find our strength. It's strange but true. We want to be strong, so we often try to appear stronger and attempt to stay tough. But we totally miss the fact that our vulnerability

> When we admit our weakness, we find our strength.

slays our weakness. And when we hide our vulnerability, our pain, the power of our past, our weaknesses grow.

God says my "power is made perfect" in the midst of our life circumstances, which are beyond what we can handle. In the midst of these circumstances, which leave us weak and broken.

The Bible is full of stories that are taking place in the midst of extraordinary, difficult situations.

Noah faces a flood.

Moses is stuck at the uncrossable Red Sea with the enemy closing in.

David faces Goliath.

Joseph is forgotten in prison.

Esther risks her life to change the mind of the king.

Paul would face one imprisonment after another.

Most of the stories we learned in Sunday school were about individuals facing situations that were completely beyond what they could handle, and it forced them to make a choice to surrender their past and present or continue to move forward pretending to have it all together.

Jesus understood better than any of us just how complex all of this would be. In John 16 he speaks about two realities that you and I need to come to grips with if we are ever going to make sense of our Plan B seasons in life.

Quick background. Jesus is about to be crucified. He's headed for the cross. He is carrying the sins of the world and he is going to the cross so that we can experience forgiveness through his substitutionary death.

He says, "I have told you these things, so that in me you may have peace. In this world you will have trouble. But take heart! I have overcome the world" (John 16:33 NIV).

Anyone interested in this peace he offers? Notice he says "in me" you may have peace. He doesn't say in church, in small group, or in this book. He clearly says, "In me." When you immerse your current reality into my reality, that is where peace is found.

And this peace is such a valuable commodity. The very next words out of Jesus' mouth remind us just why this peace is so important: "In this world you will have trouble."

And we are not talking about your-dog-pooped-on-the-floor trouble or you-locked-yourself-out-of-your-house trouble. We're talking about the kind of trouble that makes you wonder if there is a God. This is the kind of trouble, pain, or crisis that can rock you to the very core of your foundation.

We live in two overlapping realities: there is a God who is big and powerful and loves us, but we are in a world that seems as if it's falling apart.

Jesus ends this verse by saying, "Take heart for I have overcome the world."

Don't lose sight. Don't give into despair. Because Jesus has overcome the world. No matter what comes, he has overcome the world.

OVERCOMING OUR PAST

Jesus clearly says, "In this world you will have trouble, but take heart as I have overcome the world." If we separate those two statements, we have two bad theologies.

If we just take Jesus' first statement, "In this world you will have trouble," we develop a mental framework to interpret that this world stinks. Crap happens. You live and then you die. You can't do anything about it. I'm sure you've met people who have chosen this framework of thinking. They always feel like someone is out to destroy them. They feel as if life is pointless. It's a pretty miserable way to live.

We are not exempt from trouble.

But if we just take the second half of this verse, "I have overcome the world," we may think there is not going to be any trouble. If we cling only to this statement, we force ourselves to live in a false reality where we pretend that everything is great and all the charts of our life are going up and to the right. "Nothing bad is going to happen; I'm just following Jesus."

But if we take the two statements in this verse and put them together, then we have what Jesus was talking about—a complete theology.

We are not exempt from trouble. We are not exempt from hurt and brokenness, but we do have a confidence that Jesus has overcome the world and our past. There is hope in surrendering to him.

One place I have seen this played out effectively is in the Twelve-Step movement. I have had a lot of friends find freedom through the twelve steps, and I think there is a lot of biblical truth in them.

My friend Jon has been sober for almost fourteen years now after battling an addiction to drugs and alcohol for over two decades. He gives the credit for his freedom to Christ, and the practice of immersing himself into the authentic, broken community, which he calls his AA group.

One day we were talking about AA and how it has helped so many people overcome their addictions. He made a good point that it was ironic that one of the most powerful tools against one of the most powerful addictions never asks people to decide to stop doing what it is they have to stop doing.

I had never really thought about it before, but AA doesn't try to mobilize the addict's will. The addict has already tried that. They probably have decided to walk away from whatever addiction is plaguing them hundreds of times, but it never worked.

AA, on the other hand, doesn't try to mobilize their will, but rather they try to surrender their will.

If you're not familiar with the Twelve-Step program, the first steps are:

1. We admitted we were powerless over our addiction—that our lives had become unmanageable
2. *Came to believe that a Power greater than ourselves could restore us to sanity*
3. Made a decision to turn our will and our lives over to the care of God as we understood God

Millions upon millions have found strength to overcome what had rendered them helpless. And for each one of them, that healing starts with a single step: admitting that they are powerless. Why would this be the starting place? After all, the goal is to gain power and strength over a demon that has knocked us off our feet. So why start by admitting our weakness?

On the surface, it doesn't make sense. Yet this seeming impossibility is the great untapped reservoir of strength within the human heart. There is great strength in owning our deepest weaknesses.

I believe that if we try to overcome our past, our pain, our junk, our sin, on our own, it will beat us. Surrendering our will, humbling ourselves, as scary as that is, and then another kind of life becomes possible. As Jesus said, "Those who exalt themselves will be humbled, and those who humble themselves will be exalted" (Matt. 23:12).

When we think of surrender, we tend to think of a white flag. We tend to think of loss. I believe, however, Scripture teaches that in the end surrender turns out to be the only way we can win. It's the only way to be exalted by God himself.

> Scripture teaches that in the end surrender turns out to be the only way we can win.

We all know people who have become much meaner and more irritable to be around because they held on to the suffering they've endured in their past. And we've seen people who have been through similar suffering and seem to let go, rise above it, and find healing that engenders an attitude that draws others to them. How could the same suffering produce such different demeanors? Are some people lucky or blessed while others are cursed?

Some people will never get beyond the pain of their past. It will wreak havoc in their personal and professional lives because they will keep cursing their pain, and it will keep cursing them back. They will choose to believe they are inseparably attached to their past without realizing they are, in fact, making a choice to hold on to it.

They will hold on to it in one of two ways. Either they will give in to it with a self-loathing that ensures perpetual misery and failure, or they will wage an angry and desperate war against it in an effort to bury its devastation in self-denial. Either way, they will never surrender the past pain. They will hold on to the idea that they shouldn't have had to go through that pain and that life is not fair. And they will, therefore, miss out on the brand-new ending that could in fact be theirs.

Then there's a group of people who will take a different path.

They will realize their past isn't really their past. They will come to grips with the fact that their past pain is still impacting them and choose to rise above it. In an incomprehensible twist, they will surrender their pain, instead of ignoring or denying it. They will choose to be emptied of it. And in a glorious miracle, God will actually use the pain of their past to help redeem others, in effect, allowing them to find purpose in the pain.

> There is strength in letting go.

This choice isn't easy. You have to choose to do something you think you can't do. It requires a resolve that can only be found deep within your soul. But this choice does nothing less than determine your destiny.

It's the choice to let go of your desire to have life go the way you planned it. It's the choice to find hope in your hurt. It's the choice called surrender.

There is strength in letting go. There is radical power in surrender.

USING THE DEEPLY WOUNDED

Have you ever looked at your life and wondered how God could bring anything good out of it? Have you ever looked at your past and thought it would be best buried and forgotten? After all, your failings and mistakes can have no part in God's plan. Right?

Surrendering our hurt and brokenness to God is essential for many reasons. We could spend the rest of the chapter outlining the personal benefits alone. But there's one benefit that few think of. I believe that when you surrender your past to God, he can take it and use it to help others and bring Glory to himself.

God has blessed my life with a plethora of amazing friends. Two of those friends are Todd and Angie Smith. I'm so thankful

God has allowed our families to walk this path of life together. Todd and Angie have been through a lot; the way they've allowed God to use their past has been more than inspirational to me. They've taught me so much about what it looks like when you surrender your past pain, hurt, and brokenness to God.

In fact, Angie shared a story in her latest book, *Mended*, that captures this idea perfectly:

As I was driving, God spoke to me clearly, and He asked me to do something odd. I started thinking about a certain pitcher I have in my house, and as soon as it came to mind, He told me to smash it . . . Thankfully, my neighbors know me well enough to not call the police when I throw a perfectly good pitcher onto my front porch at ten o'clock at night. I watched it shatter . . . What next? I asked. Again, He was very clear. Put it back together again. What I wanted to do was go to bed, but I felt like He was meaning now, so I gathered all the pieces together and brought them in the house. I told Todd what was going on, and he took a look at the tiny shards of porcelain, knowing it was going to be a long night. I went and got the hot glue gun and sat down in the kitchen. It was hard to know where to start, but I found the lip and the handle relatively intact, and just kind of made it up as I went. I talked to the Lord while my fingers worked, and He stayed near to me. I would love to tell you that it was like a movie where everything about the moment was all sweet and perfect, but the truth is that I glued my finger to it at one point and cut myself several times. I thought about swear words that I wanted to say. But, still I kept at it. And as I worked, He let me think about my past. Mistakes I have long regretted. I began to realize that this pitcher was my life, and every piece was part of a story that He had chosen to put together. I started crying, and remembering things I thought I had forgotten. It took a long time to finish, but it was time well spent. Every nook and cranny whispered to me, until at last it stood in all its imperfection. Here you are, Angie. You are mended. You are filled with My Spirit, and I am asking you to pour yourself out. The image of my life as a broken pitcher was beautiful to me, but at the same time, it was hard to look at all of the cracks. I ran my fingers along them and told Him I wished it had been different. I wished I had always loved Him, always obeyed Him, always sought Him the way I should. I was mad at the imperfections, years wasted, gaping holes where it should be smooth. But God, my ever-gracious God, was gentle and yet convicting as He explained. *My dearest Angie. How do you think the world has seen Me? If it wasn't for the cracks, I couldn't seep out the way I do. I chose the pitcher. I chose you, just as you are.*[1]

I love that! I've spent some time thinking about this, and part of the problem is we see ourselves as pitchers that should be perfected. No wide cracks. No gaping holes. We think God intended for us to be a perfect pitcher and since we have all of this brokenness, we're now useless. The reality is God never intended for you to be a pitcher. He wanted you to be a lamp. If we put a bulb in that broken pitcher, light beams out of every imperfection.

As Jesus said, "Let your light shine before others, that they may see your good deeds and glorify your Father in heaven" (Matt. 5:16 NIV).

Another friend of mine, Michelle Myers, told me the first time she thought she was fat was when she was eight years old. She vividly recalls sitting between two of her friends at a school assembly, and noticed that her legs were bigger than both of her friends' legs. As she recalls, "I quickly sat back in my chair, holding my legs just above the seat so my legs wouldn't 'smash out.' I literally never let my legs rest on a chair the rest of elementary school unless they were totally hidden underneath my desk."

Michelle struggled with body image the rest of her growing-up years. During her freshman year of college, she contracted mononucleosis, which not only made her feel tired but also killed her appetite. For six weeks she ate barely enough to get by. When she went back to the doctor's office, she knew she had lost weight. But she had no idea how much she'd lost until she stood on the scale. "I remember the nurse gasped as she adjusted the weighted tabs on the scale. The nurse said, 'Girl, when you were here six weeks ago, you weighed 138 pounds. Today, you're only 118.'"

This new reality turned out to be a dark moment for Michelle as her lifelong battle with this particular idol took a dangerous turn. She had entered the frightening new world of anorexia nervosa.

Michelle did the math in her head there in the doctor's office. She thought, *If I lost 3.5 pounds a week without working out, how much weight could I lose if I added working out back into my schedule?*

Michelle made a vow that day that she would do whatever it took to get down to "the perfect weight"—which was far less than her present weight of 118. This new goal consumed her life. She exercised for hours each day and held herself to a very legalistic diet of just sixteen hundred calories a day. Another six weeks later, she was down to 105 pounds.

Michelle battled this sickness for years. Her extreme behavior made her feel more and more guilty, and she continued to push away from her faith. She told me, "How could God possibly use the girl who held Communion in her mouth without swallowing? I would wait until the prayer, sneak out of the aisle to the bathroom, and spit the bread and grape juice into the toilet. I couldn't even bring myself to sacrifice ten calories to remember the fact that he suffered a horrible death and sacrificed himself so I could spend eternity with him."

But on April 14, 2005, God finally got Michelle's full attention. After thirteen days without a single meal, she went for a run as part of her training for a full marathon. But at mile nineteen her vision started to blur. She tripped and came crashing to the ground. All eighty-four pounds hit the pavement and, as she remembers, "I literally felt like every brittle bone in my body cracked simultaneously."

Michelle doesn't remember how long she blacked out. But eventually she became conscious again and limped back to the car, realizing she was in desperate need of help. That day she finally admitted to friends and family members—and to God—that something was seriously wrong with her. And in that moment she began the long and slow road to recovery.

> The Bible is a story about broken people, and God's choice to love them anyway.

Michelle is just one of approximately seven million women and girls and another one million men and boys who struggle with eating disorders. Her story is being played out every day around the world in the lives of millions of people.

Michelle has a haunting past, but she refuses to allow those dark days to stay in the dark. In fact, she's spent the last decade of her life investing in other young women trying to help save them from the same destructive path she went down. She just wrote an amazing little book called *The Look That Kills*, which recounts her story and her recovery in hopes of helping other young women caught in this vicious addiction. God is using her dark days.

As author Brennan Manning put it, "Anyone God uses significantly is almost always deeply wounded." The Bible is a story about broken people, and God's choice to love them anyway. The Bible is brutally honest about people, even the people we now look up to. King David was a great king. With a great lust problem. Peter had great faith. And also stuck his foot in his mouth during important moments. God sent Jonah on a mission. And he literally ran in the opposite direction. I think the Bible makes it clear that broken people matter to God.

But we must surrender our brokenness.

What is it that will turn the people of God from a group of washed-up, hiding-out, convinced-they're-not-worthy people to a group willingly surrendered to allow God to use their past? It will be a renewal of confidence, implanted in us by this one simple truth:

We are loved by God—absolutely, unconditionally, and forever.

As Paul wrote to the Christians in Rome, "Who shall separate us from the love of Christ? Shall tribulation, or distress, or persecution, or famine, or nakedness, or peril, or sword? . . . In all these things we are more than conquerors through Him who loved us. For I am persuaded that neither death nor life, nor angels nor principalities nor powers, nor things present nor things to come, nor height nor depth, nor any other created thing, shall be able to separate us from the love of God which is in Christ Jesus our Lord" (Rom. 8:35–39 NKJV).

It is only by focusing on that truth and making it the foundation stone of our lives that God can use us and all the pieces of our past—the good, the bad, and the ugly—to minister to the struggling, lonely, fearful, hurting, discouraged, sinful people. People like us. We are, each and every one of us, insignificant people whom God has called and graced to use in a significant way.

HOPE THROUGH YOUR SCARS

When I was ten years old I got in an epic sibling fight with my then nine-year-old sister, Kristi. While the details are a bit foggy, I do remember that I had been fulfilling my obligation as the older brother to tease and torment my younger sister. She had finally had enough and decided to bring about restitution. This led into a bit of a physical altercation that prompted me to chase my sister down. I knew if I could catch her, I would come out on top. However, as we ran into the house she quickly slammed the back door in my face. My momentum carried me right through the glass door leaving me cut in several places.

One of the most intense, surprising, and hopeful scenes in Scripture is centered around scars.

She had won the battle but not the war.

Numerous stitches later, that afternoon assured that I would be fine, but there would forever be scars to mark this epic fight. For years as a kid I would proudly show off my scars with friends hoping to garner the "prize" for the biggest scar. It was proof that I was tough. It was a symbol that I had survived. I often left out the minor detail about getting beat up by my younger sister that day.

Over time, though, I became quite self-conscious of that scar. It's interesting how childhood innocence fades away into grownup mind-sets that teach us that scars are to be hidden. And not just the physical scars, but the emotional ones as well.

One of the most intense, surprising, and hopeful scenes in Scripture is centered around scars. Following his resurrection, Jesus' followers are holed up in a room, scared that their lives are in jeopardy. On top of their fear was a deep sense of sadness that they had just days earlier watched the man they had devoted their very lives to following die. With Jesus' death so many of their dreams had died.

But when they were least expecting it, Jesus shows up.

After his resurrection, Jesus appeared to his disciples. To prove his identity, he showed them his scars and invited them to touch the scars.

Can you imagine the moment?

The disciples have been through a week from hell. Their leader has been openly crucified. They have all found themselves in failure having deserted Jesus in one way or another. Their hopes and dreams seem dashed, and they haven't slept much. Their emotions have taken a roller-coaster ride from seeing the crowds yell, "Hosanna," to the fear-filled days of being threatened if they were Jesus' followers, to hearing that the body of Jesus has been buried. Now they hear the tomb is empty and that Jesus has risen. Hope tries to rise in their hearts, but they are wounded and emotionally spent.

It's against this backdrop that Jesus appears to them. The disciples were terrified and confused even further. And then Jesus offered his scars as irrefutable evidence of his identity. He's showing them he's the very same Jesus who they followed, who they had deserted, and who they had carried off to the tomb.

Just as scars on our physical bodies were once wounds, emotional scars were first wounded places in our souls. All wounds need to heal, whether it is the wounds we have inflicted upon others or our own wounds, and Jesus identifies with our woundedness, offering us healing through his scars.

When Jesus offered his hands and feet as evidence of his identity, he was showing his disciples a few other things as well.

First, he was showing them that suffering is absolutely necessary. Collecting scars is part of the human journey. Jesus was proof that even the innocent don't escape suffering. If suffering and scars could have been avoided, surely Jesus ought to have escaped.

Second, when he shows them his scars, he is showing them that he was healed from his wounds. He's not bleeding from them, and he's no longer in pain. I can't help but wonder if in much the same way, we are to offer our scars to the world as evidence of our identity, our life story, and the healing power of Christ in our life.

The wounds of our past have inevitably left scars. But the scars are only there to remind us that we are human. That we did survive. Those scars can be a reminder of the unique way we can embrace our past and in doing so shine the light of hope in a unique way into others' lives.

WITH GOD

The other day while driving, I was wondering why God uses people to represent him. Why does he use us for the work he wants to do in the world? Why would he assign us to be his representatives? People have a consistent, faithful track record of unfaithfulness, and we are notorious for seeking our own ego-driven, self-centered, materialistic desires. So why does God use us to get his work done when we are more than likely to delay all the good he wants to accomplish?

> He uses us broken people to show us just how reliant on him we are.

I find my own life to be inconsistent and, yes, even when I'm faithful to do what God has called me to do, there is always that lurking reality that in the next step I can and probably will do as much harm as good.

So why use broken, messed-up people? Why the continual battle with us and with ourselves to be emptied of our past, our selfishness, our pride, our insecurity, in order for the work to be done? Why not use the angels to do the work? There are angels doing tasks all throughout the Bible and, as far as I can tell, they did their work exactly as they were told and with no complaint.

Perhaps he uses us broken people to show us just how reliant on him we are. To illuminate his perfection with our imperfection. To show others that, despite all the brokenness of their past and present, he still has the power and capacity to lead them into good works and to transform their lives.

While these reasons make sense to me, I think there's a bigger reason. Maybe he simply wants to be *with* us. And I think we've been created to be *with* him.

In the very beginning of creation, we see that God created a garden, a place, where he could "be with" both Adam and Eve. In Genesis 3 we get the idea that God would often walk with them in the garden: "Then the man and his wife heard the sound of the LORD God as he was walking in the garden in the cool of the day" (v. 8 NIV).

Walking is something you do with somebody you care about, like a friend with a friend, or a child with a parent. Two people in love would go for a walk. When Brandi and I were first dating, we would often meet late at night after we were done studying and walk around our college campus. This would be the same walk that earlier in the day I would be complaining about "how far I have to walk to class." But I didn't complain when I was walking with her. We just walked and talked about everything.

Last week I got a little sideways with one of my boys. He was mad at me for making him turn off a video game he had been playing most of the day. I told him I needed him to walk down to the creek with me. When we got there he asked, "Dad, why did you need me to come with you? You totally could have walked down here by yourself."

"Sure I could, but why would I walk alone when I can walk with you?" I responded.

As we headed back, we had taken about twenty steps or so when I felt a little hand reach up and take my hand. All the way back we just held hands and never spoke a word to each other.

When we got back I told Brandi I just had the best walk with Gage. She asked what we talked about. "Nothing," I said, "but my heart is so full right now."

It's not really about the walk, is it? It's about being with someone.

This God, this God of the Bible, is a God who wants to be with you. You were made to walk with God. You were made for a "with God" life.

And this idea continues throughout the Gospels in Jesus' life. In John 15, Jesus said, "I am the vine; you are the branches. If a man remains in me and I in him, he will bear much fruit; apart from me you can do nothing" (v. 5 NIV).

You were made to walk with God.

I am the vine; you are the branch and you're going to bear fruit. You're going to do wonderful things in your life, but your job is not to try to do wonderful things; your job is to abide in the vine, which is Jesus, from one moment to the next. "If you don't do that," Jesus says, "nothing much will come out of your life."

There's just one thing a branch is supposed to do: remain. Abide. Be with.

As we prepare to surrender everything that we are so God can use every part of our lives, I think it's important to remember that God wants to walk *with* us before he works *through* us.

God says in Micah 6:8 that what he desires for us is "to act justly and to love mercy and to walk humbly with your God" (NIV). He wants us to "be with" him. In fact, he promises that he will never leave us nor forsake us.

Because of this promise, in those times that God feels distant from me, when I wonder if he really cares, I have to recognize that as a feeling and not reality.

My life can be a mess. I often tell my church that if they knew just how big of a mess I was, they probably wouldn't want me to be their pastor. After about thirty years of trying to follow Jesus, I keep losing him in the pain of my past and the busyness of my present.

For as long as I can remember, I have wanted to be a godly person. I've wanted God to use my life to make a difference. Yet when I look in the rearview mirror of my life, what I see, mostly, is a broken, littered path with mistakes and failure.

I have had some amazing moments of closeness to God that I wouldn't exchange for any amount of money, but I long for the continuing presence of Jesus. The reality is that most of the moments of my life seem hopelessly tangled in a web of obligations and distractions and the repeated moments of licking my own wounds. I say I want to walk with Jesus, but most of the time, however, I feel like I am running away from Jesus into the arms of my own self-centered, ego-driven, materialistic desires.

I want desperately to know God better. I want to be consistent. Right now the only consistency in my life is my inconsistency. There is an alarming gap between who I want to be and who I actually am.

There's too much "me trying" and not enough "me abiding." I'm renewing my commitment to walk with Jesus. To "be with" this God who can and will bring healing and purpose to the totality of my life. It's here and only here that I'll truly be able to let hope in.

My greatest hope is not fame, comfort, wealth, or power. These will ultimately still make me feel empty. My greatest hope is much deeper.

My greatest hope is for meaning and purpose. And letting hope in happens when I begin to not just tolerate my past but embrace my past, surrendering it to God's higher purposes.

CHOICE THREE:

CHOOSING TO TRUST RATHER THAN PLEASE

7

TRUSTING VS. PLEASING

I ran my very first half marathon recently. I've never enjoyed running. In fact, I pretty much hate it. I get tired driving thirteen miles across town, so the idea of actually running thirteen miles has never excited me. But in a moment of weakness, I allowed a friend to talk me into signing up for an April race.

I started training in January. There is only one thing I hate more than running, and that is cold weather—combine the two and I am completely miserable. So in order to avoid running in the cold, I decided to train indoors. My first day at the track was pretty rough. The YMCA I'm a member of is made up primarily of senior adults. I like this gym a lot better than the gyms full of the young and the beautiful. Working out with people more than twice my age is good for my self-esteem.

But then it happened. About the moment I was feeling pretty good about blowing past the people on the track with their walkers, a woman who was at least seven, maybe eight months pregnant blew past me. She didn't just lap me once either. I felt like every time I turned around, there she was again.

So I decided I would abandon the track for a treadmill. The

treadmill was located in a warm environment and in close proximity to a television. But the treadmill didn't go anywhere.

Regardless of how hard and far I ran, I never felt I was making any progress.

There was sweat, there was deep breathing, there was exhaustion, but when I stepped off the treadmill, I was in the same place I had started. And this was only the first day of training.

I eventually made it to April and finished the race, but it's safe to say, I probably won't train indoors again for a while.

THE SPIRITUAL TREADMILL

Trevor is a good pastor friend who has been part of a particular denomination for almost forty years. It's a good denomination, but over the years, it has occasionally shown signs of leaning toward a works-based salvation. While having lunch one day, I could tell that my friend was overwhelmed. When I inquired about his tired appearance, he replied, "I've been busy working for God for nearly four decades and I'm exhausted."

> Many of us wrestle with trying to please God with our good deeds.

Tears started welling up in the corner of Trevor's eyes. "Pete, do you ever wonder how much is enough? How good is good enough?"

I just listened.

"Most of my ministry has been spent living in fear that I'm not good enough for God. From day to day I question whether or not he really loves me. And if I'm honest, most of my ministry has been fueled by this fear; and the harder I try, the more I feel like I'm failing."

My friend is hardly alone in his struggle. Many of us wrestle with trying to please God with our good deeds. I call this the "spiritual treadmill," a condition that causes us to work harder and harder and harder and never feel like we're really making any progress toward pleasing God.

Make no mistake: the spiritual treadmill is a trap. It's a lifestyle that leads us into believing that freedom will exist at the next level. It causes us to think that if we could do just a little more for God, then we'd know he loves and accepts us. But once we reach our goal, the spiritual bar gets raised. We end up falling short and feel the need to make up for our failures.

Time and time again, life teaches that we'll never be good enough. Our lives tell the tale over and over again: work-based religion doesn't work.

The thing is, religion sniffs out the insecurities that we wrestle with and lures us into thinking we can make up our past failures and mishaps. Religion whispers, "If you would just give more. Show up more. Serve more. Pray more. Read more. Memorize more. Evangelize more. Sing more. Then, and only then, God will love you. At the very least, he'll love you a little more."

And oftentimes, we fall for religion's lie and earn God's love. We attempt to embrace a rhythm of life that wears us out. We hop on the spiritual treadmill and we run. We run and run and run. But the more we run, the more exhausted we become. Every day, we wonder, wish, hope we've done enough to earn his love and grace.

THE MOST IMPORTANT THING ABOUT YOU

Our failures and fears from the past deceivingly seem to be recorded in the very cells of our bodies. As much as we long to move forward, there's something that keeps drawing us back.

We look for the love we missed.

We fear the blows we cannot forget.

We work hard to earn the acceptance that has somehow eluded us again and again.

My kids think they want a lot of stuff—a new pair of tennis shoes, a video game, and football gloves. But what they're really looking for is attention, acceptance, appreciation, and affection. I call these the 4 A's.

When we were children, we were looking for the exact same thing. Every child, whether they realize it or not, dreams of having these 4 A's met. Some of us were given too little attention, while others were given too much attention. Parents who overprized us were instilling needs rather than fulfilling them like they thought. Needs unfulfilled and under-fulfilled become exaggerated later.

I find it interesting that a lot of people don't even recall what happened in their childhood, almost as though they've intentionally blocked it out. We don't recall how we were treated until we get into an adult relationship and see the ramifications. All it takes is a partner treating us like our parents did for the floodgates of our past to come wide open.

Years ago I was meeting with a couple who was having a difficult time in their marriage. There were several issues, but one of the big ones was their communication—or lack thereof. As we started to explore a little bit, it seemed apparent that the husband had given up years ago being able to have a rational conversation with his wife and chose to simply withdraw. He told me, "Pete, I can't say the least little thing to her without her blowing up. If I mention how we need to work with the kids on something or we need to tackle a certain home improvement project, she just blows up. She thinks everything is a statement against her."

As I started to explore some of these issues with his wife, it became clear that she had grown up in a home where her father never thought she had done enough. He was constantly correcting her and reprimanding her. She had been dealt very low levels of the third A, which is appreciation.

The more we can remember how our needs were under- or over-fulfilled as children, the more likely we are to grieve the past and let go of it so we can meet other adults not as figures from our past but as real people in the present.

This is true in our relationship with God. Few people truly see God for God. What they see is a version of God that's been created by figures from their past who didn't give them the attention, acceptance, appreciation, and affection they longed for. We project on God the inconsistencies of our past.

Author A. W. Tozer once wrote in *The Knowledge of the Holy*, "What comes into our minds when we think about God is the most important thing about us."[1] We need to let go of our past so we don't project it on God, which will have devastating results on our life. For every misconception your past has projected on God, there's a corresponding consequence.

If something from your past makes you see God as an impatient father withholding his love from you until you finally become "good enough," you may never stop jumping through unnecessary hoops, trying to make him happy.

If you see him as a cosmic cop waiting for you to screw up, you'll spend your life walking on eggshells and doubting his love.

If you see him as a heavenly concierge whose main concern is your comfort, you may resent him when he doesn't do what you want him to do.

In order to move forward, we need to let go of our past.

TWO DISTINCT PATHS

Up to this point in the book we've looked at two important choices: (1) Will you transform or transfer (2) Will you choose to be okay with not being okay? We know our past is impacting us, and hopefully we're getting to a place where we can humble ourselves and ask for help and healing. But what's next?

There are two distinct paths that we can take in the so-called Christian life. A couple of years ago I read a book called *True Faced* where the authors talked about two distinct paths we could potentially take.

Path One: This is the path of pleasing God or "working on my sin" so I can achieve an intimate relationship with God. This sounds very, well, Christian. It's all about selling out, trying harder, and committing more.

> We focus on sin management—in essence, behavioral modification.

But over time this path will make you cynical and tired because it's characterized by self-effort and one's own goal, or focus, in sinning less. One of the tendencies we have in Christianity today is that we focus on sin management—in essence, behavioral modification. While there are several problems with this path, the biggest I see is that the Gospels make it clear that Jesus doesn't want to edit behaviors; rather, he wants to change hearts.

Path Two: This is the path of trusting God with my sin instead of trying to please him by not sinning, which is the goal of the first. It may seem subtle, but this path is drastically different from the first. On this path I'm simply living out who God says I am.

While choosing path two seems like a no-brainer, in my experience, most of us choose to spend our time here on this earth exploring the guilt-ridden, failure-producing traps of path one. Path two doesn't seem as spiritual or as heroic. And beyond that, the real reason we're drawn to path one is because of our past.

Remember, we've been hardwired for attention, acceptance, appreciation, and affection, and since we've spent our life trying to earn these 4 A's, it seems natural to project that on God and fall into the routine of trying to please him.

And we're not the first to feel this pull toward path one. In fact, the apostle Paul goes to great lengths to help the early Christians from making the same mistake. Their past—living the religious life of a Jew—set them up to go running down path one.

In the early church Gentiles were forced to live like Jews in order to be acceptable to them. Behind this social crisis, however, a more fundamental theological issue was at stake: Was the truth of the gospel the basis for determining fellowship between Jewish and Gentile Christians, or was it it the law?

Jewish Christians were taking salvation, which comes through faith in Jesus and what he did on the cross alone, and were adding to it other rules and regulations. In essence, they said that circumcision is needed along with Jesus for salvation.

Jesus + circumcision = salvation

Now we look at that and think that's silly. You don't have to be circumcised to be a Christian. But the reality is that almost every generation and every culture has been tempted to add something to that equation. For instance:

Jesus + being immersed in water = salvation
Jesus + doing Communion a certain way = salvation
Jesus + voting Republican (or Democrat) = salvation
Jesus + church membership = salvation

There are dozens and dozens of things that we've tried to force into that equation. And each time we do that, we are mixing law and grace—and becoming dangerously close to turning religion into an idol.

Religion tends to want to complicate what God has made simple. Early Jewish Christians had created a sort of equation that still exists today in most religious circles. In fact, this equation is pretty consistent among all the major religions of the world.

More Right Behavior + Less Wrong Behavior = Godliness

This theology comes with a significant problem, because it sets us up to fail and to live in hypocrisy. Our determination to please God traps us in a formula that will leave us living exhausted and fake, and even if we do experience some success in transformation, we'll become prideful and judgmental.

The apostle Paul tackled this issue head on in his letter to the Galatians: "We Jews know that we have no advantage of birth over 'non-Jewish sinners.' We know very well that we are not set right with God by rule-keeping but only through personal faith in Jesus Christ" (Gal. 2:15 MSG).

Paul went on to say that the Jews had a great system of rules but Jesus still needed to come to save them anyway. Obeying their rules and being good didn't work. "For some of you your entire Christian life has been about ... 'trying to be good'" (2:18). Pleasing God is a great longing, but it cannot be our primary motivation or it will imprison our hearts. When our motive is trusting God, our focus is then living out who God says I am. As a follower of Christ you have received a new heart. You have a new identity. You've already been changed and now you get to mature into who you already are.

As a follower of Christ you have received a new heart.

A few chapters later, Paul addressed circumcision, which was the main rule of his day that many believed was needed for salvation. "Those who are trying to force you to be circumcised want to look good to others. . . . And even those who advocate circumcision don't keep the whole law themselves. . . . It doesn't matter whether we have been circumcised or not. What counts is whether we have been transformed into a new creation" (6:12–13, 15).

Paul was saying that the central issue is not about a list of rules. We can't achieve godliness through rule following, as we're no match against sin. It's not about working a little harder, doing a little more.

The central issue is what God is doing. What counts is the inward transformation that he alone can do in our hearts, which truly heals the wounds of our past and allows us to start living the life he created us to live.

SOLVING MY ISSUES

For me, I'm often tempted by the thought that I'm only three issues away from really being used by God to do something significant. My three issues include the following:

1. My temper. If I could just learn to control my emotions at all times.
2. My thought life. If I could just get to the place where I never had a single lustful thought. I bet it's possible. I'm going to work harder at that.
3. My love. There are still some people who drive me absolutely crazy. They're usually judgmental religious people, but I understand that if I hate the haters, I become like them. I've got to try harder to love them.

And then I'll spend countless hours uselessly trying to solve those and many other similar issues. But the reality is I will never solve all my issues. The *intention* not to sin is not the same as the *power* not to sin.

In fact, I kind of hope you and I don't solve our issues because then we would become self-sufficient. The goal of spiritual maturity is not for us to get all of our stuff "solved." We never will. The goal is to learn to depend on, to trust, what God says is true about us, so that together we can begin dealing with stuff. We will not know God's power until we give up on our power—which is actually no power at all.

> The *intention* not to sin is not the same as the *power* not to sin.

This thinking is counterintuitive because all the sensors from our past are alerting us to head down path one, to earn attention, acceptance, appreciation, and affection.

Let's think about it this way: In this life, those of us who have trusted in Christ will have sin issues, and we will always have the identity God gave us. They are constants, and unchanging realities.

Pleasing God = working on my sin issues.
Trusting God = believing I am who God says I am.

We need to ask ourselves which of these two constants defines our life focus? Which offers us the hope of experiencing the other? If we opt for the top line (path one), we will never experience the bottom line (path two). But if we focus on the bottom line, we will experience unparalleled transformation regarding our sin issues.

In order to resolve our sin issues, we must begin by trusting who God says we are. God did not design us to conquer sin on our own or heal the wounds from our past on our own. As the writer of Hebrews put it, "And without faith it is impossible to please God" (11:6 NIV).

Did you see the two paths in this verse? There is the path of trusting and the path of pleasing. Trusting God pleases God. If our primary motive is pleasing God, we never please him enough, and we never learn to trust. That's because life on this road is all about my striving, my effort, my ability to make something happen.

But if our primary motive is trusting God, we find out that he is incredibly pleased with us. So pleasing God is actually a by-product of trusting God.

HE LOVES ME, HE LOVES ME NOT

As a kid I really enjoyed school. My favorite part of the day was recess, of course. I attended Park Avenue Christian school, and every afternoon at one thirty our teachers led us across the road to the playground so we could let our energy out. Recess wasn't the most educational part of the day, but it's often where we learn about life. It's where I discovered that girls had cooties, that knock-knock jokes are timeless, that four-leaf clovers are lucky, and that I really could fly if I swung high enough.

This was the stage in our lives when we started developing what we believed were strange feelings for the opposite sex, and we had no idea how to communicate those feelings.

One day I was playing with my friend Angie, a beautiful red-haired girl who had a crush on my friend Jason. Angie was holding a flower and slowly pulling off one petal at a time saying, "He loves me; he loves me not. He loves me; he loves me not." With each proclamation of Jason's love for her or his non-love for her, Angie pulled another petal from her flower. As you probably know, the point of this silly game is to arrive at the final petal on a "He loves me!" Because, of course, that was the universal "sign" that the other person actually loved you.

Yes, that game is ridiculous and childish, but in some ways, as Christians, we still play it if we choose to go down path one.

Somewhere along the way we've reduced the discovery of God's love to something almost as random as those flower petals. Each day is full of random hoops we must jump through and bars we must jump over in hopes that today may be the day we finally earn God's love.

I recently had a meeting with a couple who was demanding to meet with me and one of our campus pastors at Cross Point. The couple had heard the campus pastor give his testimony at Cross Point, which included an extramarital affair, a painful event that led him to resign from ministry. During the long journey toward healing, this pastor went through almost five years of counseling and restoration. For him the process was grueling, life changing, and ultimately, what saved his marriage. He had recently come on staff with us to pastor one of our campuses.

This couple was disgusted that we had hired this pastor, which is why they wanted to meet with us. According to them, the pastor's past sin had disqualified him from serving in ministry. And during our meeting, they fired at us one question after another: How do you expect the people of this church to ever trust you again? How do we know you won't do this again? How could you have ever done something so bad, if you are a Christian? We understand if you hadn't been a Christian, but you say you were when you did these terrible things.

Sadly, this particular couple could not wrap their minds around the concept that God had restored this pastor through his grace. They felt if he had committed this particular sin before he was a Christian, forgiveness was possible. But since he'd committed it as a Christian, there was no hope of God using him in ministry again.

After they left that evening, I sat at my desk discouraged. It's hard for me to understand why we have to put such limits on what God can do in and through our lives with his grace. Why do we feel the need to put stipulations on what God has so freely given us? Why are we so determined to keep ourselves and those around us locked up in who they used to be?

We attract people to Christianity by telling them that it's the only world religion where someone (Jesus) comes along and pays the penalty for you. Every other world religion is about *do*, while Christianity is about *done*. However, once we cast the bait and a person bites, the story quickly changes. What was once a story about acceptance and grace transforms to a story about performance and conformity.

There is a term that is often used in theological circles called "Galatianism." According to Dr. C. I. Scofield in *The Scofield Reference Bible*, "The Galatian error had two forms, both of which are refuted. The first is the teaching that obedience to the law is mingled with faith as the ground of the sinner's justification; the second, that the justified believer is made perfect by keeping the law."[2]

We attract people to Christianity by telling them that it's the only world religion where someone (Jesus) comes along and pays the penalty for you.

Galatianism takes on many forms, but it comes down to the same basic principle: justification—forgiveness and redemption—is initially received by faith but is then sustained by human efforts to keep the law. It's an attempt to mix both law and grace, and it tries to convince us that grace ends at salvation. I call it the bait and switch. It simply fuels and perpetuates the "he loves me, he loves me not" game.

In Christianity, God actually shows up and says, "You've done enough. I got it. This is not about what you do; it's about what I did. I got it. Because in the midst of your not being good enough, in the midst of your sin, I went ahead and paid the price."

Sometime I just sit and think about all of the messes that I've made. I think about how many times I've made poor choices. I think about how many times I've lost my temper. How many times I've failed to be patient. How many times I've had lustful thoughts. And I'm so thankful for a God who can take this mess I've made and can breathe restoration and redemption to it.

Over time you'll discover, if you haven't already, that path one (trying to please God) is a tiresome system of manmade dos and don'ts, woulds and shoulds, incapable to change human lives but tragically capable of exhausting and devastating them.

THE DISTANCE TO GOD

Alece had come to see me because her second husband was accusing her of having a relationship with a guy at work. I asked her if the accusation was true, not really expecting for her to be honest with me. I had no reason to believe yet that Alece was a dishonest person. I just figured she was fighting so hard for marriage that she wouldn't be honest about what she had done or not done.

But she was honest: "I'm not having a sexual relationship with anyone else, but there is a guy I've been emotionally connected with at work." Her story was a bit surprising to me, as she actually had a good marriage. In fact, the "good marriage" was part of the problem. Alece had a history of being her own worst enemy. She had systematically self-imploded every healthy relationship she had ever been in, including but not limited to her first marriage, which ended in divorce because of her infidelity.

We met several times over the next several weeks while she was somewhat in crisis mode. I tried to help Alece connect the dots between her past and present. I tried to help her see how the lack of attention, acceptance, appreciation, and affection had made her act out in unhealthy ways. I tried to help her see how she was stuck in her past and how it had created this vicious cycle of self-loathing.

But she couldn't see it.

Maybe she didn't want to see it.

She was comfortable with her past. So no matter how I took aim at her worthlessness and shame, they were clearly immovable objects. She looked tired and distant, but I couldn't help feeling as though I was in a tug-of-war match with Goliath. I was trying to help her see how Jesus could take away her shame, but she was determined to hold on.

> We believe God loves us, but we also believe he's disappointed in us.

Alece was stuck on path one and couldn't find her way out. The voices of shame spoke loudly into her mind. This shame can speak with complete confidence and still be an absolute lie. I tried telling her that she couldn't trust it. But she kept walking down the path of trying to please God.

I don't know for sure that she was actually more comfortable with shame than grace, but I do know she thought she deserved it. This shame can't be trusted.

One of the biggest problems in Christianity today is that so many Christians see their sin as a gigantic cavern that is creating distance from God. We believe God loves us, but we also believe he's disappointed in us. That our imperfections, and our sin are causing this growing gap in our relationship with Jesus.

There's an illustration that has been used for decades to help people understand our need for Jesus. Imagine you're standing on the edge of a cliff and God is on the other side. There's no way for you to get to the other side, to cross the middle. Sin separates us from God. You can yell back and forth, but it's a deeply unsatisfying relationship.

This abyss represents sin. So the question is, how do you get to God? The answer is, you don't. Not unless you can find some way to remove the sin from your life. But the problem is, because you're human, not only can you not do anything about the sin you've already committed but you're actually contributing to this gap on a daily basis.

This is an accurate depiction of someone who doesn't have life in Christ. However, the illustration makes no sense if you're a Christian, and yet this is how so many Christians are living. There is a cavern of sin that separates you from God, and you feel distant from him as if your salvation never took place.

> Living for acceptance and love is slavery; living from acceptance and love is freedom.

Because we have Jesus in us, it's not God on one side and us on the other, both of us staring at this gap of sin, wondering what to do. What if, instead, we stood in front of our sin, taking full responsibility yet realizing Jesus is standing next to us and we are trusting his provision for the very sin we've just committed? What if we truly believed we were without condemnation? What if grace really was that strong?

We then notice that there's no longer the abyss but two paths we can choose to take. Through Jesus, God is now asking us similar questions:

What if I take away any element of fear or condemnation, judgment, or rejection?

What if I tell them I love them and will always love them, that there's nothing they can do to make me love them any more or any less?

What if I tell them they don't have to put on masks, that it's okay to not be okay?

What if they were convinced that bad circumstances aren't my way of evening the score for taking advantage of me?

What if I tell them that even if they run to the ends of the earth and do the most horrible, unthinkable things, that when they come back, I'd receive them with tears and a huge party?

Grace is believing that against all odds and past history, we are loved and chosen, and we do not have to get it all together. It's not the absence of trouble but the presence of God. It's making contact with something unseen, way bigger than we could ever imagine in our wildest dreams. It's realizing the abyss of our past is no longer holding us back from God.

Living for acceptance and love is slavery; living from acceptance and love is freedom.

So which path will you journey down? Will you seek to trust or please?

I want to live a life where I have to lean on God's grace rather than trying the journey alone to reach him.

8

SURPRISED BY GOD

The other night I checked in on my son Brewer, and he was just lying in bed with his eyes open, well past his bedtime. I sat down on the end of his bed and asked him what he was still doing up. He said he was too worried.

"Son, you're six years old. What do you have to be worried about?"

He said, "I'm afraid someone is watching me, Dad."

I went on to reassure him that nobody was watching him. His blinds were shut and I checked in the closet and under the bed and it was all clear. As I turned to walk out of the room he asked, "Well, what about God?"

His question led me into a ten-minute explanation about the difference between God watching you and Santa Claus watching you. Somewhere along the way he had confused the two (easy to do in our culture) and felt as though God was watching him to catch him doing something wrong.

Our conversation reminded me of the time I was at the mall and overheard a mother of an unruly preschooler, who was pulling clothes off a hanger in one of the stores, threaten her daughter with, "Stop that right now. Don't you know God sees you doing that?" While the mom's statement may be true, she was using that fact to plant the idea in her daughter's mind that there was a God in heaven watching her every move, just waiting to catch her in a bad act and pounce on her. I can only imagine how that will impact that little girl's thoughts on God as she grows older.

What comes into your mind when you think about God?

Your answer to that question will have huge implications for how you begin to let go of your past and let hope in.

WHAT IS GOD LIKE?

There is a dangerous temptation many of us face to think we've got God all figured out. I've noticed that I tend to get myself into all kinds of trouble when I make assumptions about how God might feel or act. We like to feel certain that we know how God feels, how he thinks, how he moves, and we leave no room for mystery or questions.

> There is a dangerous temptation many of us face to think we've got God all figured out.

We walk a fine line when we assume that God must think and feel and respond as we do. God is "other," unlike us in so many different ways. In fact, so much of Jesus' ministry here on earth was spent telling stories about God, which shocked the religious groups of his day. These parables Jesus would tell often show us a God who will constantly surprise us, turning over any preconceived notions we have about who he is or what he will do.

Consider the parable of the prodigal son in Luke 15, a story Jesus shared in response to the religious leaders' beliefs on who

God accepts and who he rejects. The story is about a lost soul being welcomed home with open arms, and is a revealing picture of what God is like—a picture that contradicted so many images that had been painted of him by the Jews of his time. It also paints a picture of God that contradicts so many of today's God images that churches and theologies create.

One of the reasons this story is so rich is it paints a beautiful picture of what God is truly like, erasing so many of the distortions we've picked up over time. There are times when I read this story that I just weep at the pure goodness of God.

Jesus began the story with a younger son asking his father for his inheritance. In Jesus' time, when a father was on his death bed, he typically would call his sons to his bedside and discuss giving him his share of the wealth. This was a time-honored tradition, a practice rooted in culture.

But Jesus' story included a son that basically said, "Hey Dad, I know you have worked your tail off for most of your life to make a living and provide for our family, and I know that you know that I will probably blow all of this money on some really stupid stuff, and I know this may seem like I really can't wait for you to die to get my hands on your money, but I was wondering if I could have my piece of the pie a little early?"

Now Jesus' audience was listening to this and were probably laughing. They were probably thinking, *Yeah, right. I know what I'd tell my son if he asked me that.* A request like that would have caused most traditional Middle Eastern fathers of Jesus' time to strike their sons across their faces and driven them out of the house.

But the father in Jesus' story does something no Middle Eastern father would ever do: he actually gives his son his inheritance early. I imagine Jesus' audience gasping. "What? No ordinary dad would do that!" Which was exactly Jesus' point. The Middle Eastern father in Jesus' story is no ordinary dad, and more important, the God (or heavenly Father) he represents, is no ordinary God.

The religious people in Jesus' day desperately needed to be reminded of that truth, and I believe many of us also need to be reminded of this. Jesus was painting a picture of God that scraped against the grain of that culture's belief and tradition. He introduces us to a God who will let us make our own mistakes.

Many people wonder why God didn't simply create humans as spirit beings without human nature. Why did he first make us physical—from the dust of the earth in Genesis—then offer us eternal life only if we trust in his Son, Jesus? If God can do all things, why didn't he just create us with perfect character?

Of course, God could have done that—if he had been willing to create us without the personal character we need for making personal choices. God had a choice about how humans would be created. He could have made us to function like programmed robots whose only course of action is to carry out the instructions of their maker. But instead he chose to create us like him, capable of making choices that are limited only by our knowledge and character.

So we have this God who is constantly forming our character, and part of the way that happens is by us making our own choices.

A GOD WHO RUNS

Jesus continued his story by describing how the younger son, the prodigal son, takes his inheritance, leaves home, and makes a series of horrible choices in his life—choices that leave him empty and struggling: "After he had spent everything, there was a severe famine in that whole country, and he began to be in need.

So he went and hired himself out to a citizen of that country, who sent him to his fields to feed pigs. He longed to fill his stomach with the pods that the pigs were eating, but no one gave him anything" (Luke 15:14–16 NIV).

The prodigal son is afraid to go home to his father because he is afraid his poor decisions and running from the father has cost him his relationship. He is afraid he has no leverage to negotiate his acceptance. His past is too costly for his father to forgive. Instead, he devises a plan: "How many of my father's hired men have food to spare, and here I am starving to death! I will set out and go back to my father and say to him: Father, I have sinned against heaven and against you. I am no longer worthy to be called your son; make me like one of your hired men" (vv. 17–19 NIV).

Does his plan sound at all vaguely familiar to you? It should. It seems we're all in negotiation with God to try to get his help in exchange for our good behavior. We promise to do what we're told, and we expect God to forgive us. This is a straightforward business arrangement, and we fully expect it to work. Meanwhile, we talk about being God's as if we're family.

But in our performance-for-forgiveness arrangement, things don't operate on grace. As Jesus completed the story, "But while he was still a long way off, his father saw him and was filled with compassion for him; he ran to his son, threw his arms around him and kissed him" (v. 20 NIV).

What an amazing picture of our God! The father runs to the son. In the ancient Middle Eastern culture, men did not run. Respected men, landowners, people of wealth and dignity would never be caught running in public. It was beneath them. If

> Jesus introduces us to a God who will let us make our own mistakes.

something was needed, if something was urgent, they would send a servant running.

But I believe this father realizes how his son will be welcomed by the village when he returns in failure. He knows what the village has planned for the boy, and it's not pretty. The father thinks that if he is able to achieve reconciliation with his son in public, no one in the village will treat him badly.

So the father takes the bottom edge of his long robes in his hand and runs to welcome his pig-herding son, grabs him, and kisses him. Out of his own outlandish compassion, he empties himself, assumes the form of a servant, and runs to reconcile his estranged son.

Jesus reminds us that there is a heavenly Father who is running us down.

This scene reminds me of a passage about Jesus himself in Philippians: "Your attitude should be the same as that of Christ Jesus: Who, being in very nature God, did not consider equality with God something to be grasped, but made himself nothing, taking the very nature of a servant, being made in human likeness. And being found in appearance as a man, he humbled himself and became obedient to death—even death on a cross!" (Phil. 2:5–8 NIV).

It's easy in our religious culture to start to think that this life is all about us "running to the Father," that we're the ones who are working and obeying to get to the father. But Jesus reminds us that there is a heavenly Father who is running us down. He reaches out to us through the person of Jesus Christ.

This story wouldn't have been near as amazing if the son had taken off running for the father. It's not amazing that we love God. Why wouldn't we?

What is amazing is that God loves us. He chose us. He ran to us.

And he continues to run you down today.

THE JOY OF RESTORATION

Jesus' audience continued to listen to him tell the story of the prodigal son, and they had been surprised so far, but now they were thinking, *Well, the dad let his son make his own choice. He was so overwhelmed when his son came home that he actually ran to him, but we know how this story is going to end.*

From the Jerusalem Talmud, it is known that the Jews during the time of Jesus had a method of punishing any Jewish boy who lost the family inheritance to Gentiles. It was called the "qetsatsah ceremony." Such a violator of community expectations would face the qetsatsah ceremony if he dared return to his home village.

The ceremony was simple: The villagers would bring a large jar, fill it with burned corn, and break it in front of the guilty individual. While doing this, the community would shout, "So-and-so is cut off from his people." From that point on, the village would have nothing to do with them.

This was a religious ceremony designed to publicly embarrass and humiliate the person guilty of wrongdoing. And the people listening to this story are waiting for this ending. Sure the dad forgave the son, but the village is going to give the boy what he deserves. They're not going to overlook his dark past. They're not going to allow him to just forget where he was or who he had been. But an amazing thing happens: the father trumps the humiliating and convicting ceremony by establishing his own. "The father said to his servants, 'Quick! Bring the best robe and put it on him.

Put a ring on his finger and sandals on his feet. Bring the fattened calf and kill it. Let's have a feast and celebrate. For this son of mine was dead and is alive again; he was lost and is found.' So they began to celebrate" (Luke 15:22–24 NIV).

He does something his audience is not familiar with doing: wiping his son's slate clean. He says, "I know my son blew it. I know he made some horrible decisions. But this is between me and him. He's not an embarrassment to me. You can come over to the house tomorrow, but instead of a ceremony of rejection, we're participating in the joy of a restoration."

FULLY RESTORED

These symbols prove full forgiveness and restoration of the son to his prior status. The robe is a sign of great distinction, the ring the sign of authority, the sandals a luxury (only slaves were barefooted), and the slaughter of the fattened calf the sign of an important celebration in the family.

> Most people who know shame from their past are horribly uncomfortable with the idea of receiving honor.

The idea of God honoring you or celebrating you is almost too much to take in, isn't it? How could someone who knows us so well bestow honor on us. God honored us.

Does that make you squirm like it does me?

Most people who know shame from their past are horribly uncomfortable with the idea of receiving honor. It is hard to be honored when you don't feel very honorable. When you work hard and do well, no one minds a little recognition. But screw up and receive praise? That can be hard to take.

Yet this is the way of God's kingdom. It's called grace. Leave your discomfort at the door and get used to it. Be amazed. Just say, "Thank you" as you head down the path of trusting God. This is the only door; there is no back alley through which you can enter. If you want Jesus, you must be willing to accept the honor that goes with the relationship.

This grace and forgiveness Jesus portrayed through the father is shocking. It's unlike anything we've ever experienced. In church it seems as though we are offered grace and forgiveness, but there are strings attached. This is not only radical grace, but complete restoration.

Too often the church today wants to offer limited grace, conditional grace, strings-attached grace.

"You're forgiven, *but* we're going to keep an eye on you."

"You're welcome back in the church, *but* you'll never be able to be in ministry again."

"Your past is your past, but we're going to remind you of it to make sure you stay in line."

But according to God, sin does not make you second-class. When he looks at you, he doesn't see a prodigal, a servant, or a screwup. Instead, he sees his son, his daughter.

He doesn't see your past, but you—whole, forgiven, restored, completely.

I wish we could give you a brand-new beginning but that's impossible. Your past can't be totally erased. However, your past can be restored. Even if you can't have a brand-new beginning, you can have a brand-new ending.

God's grace is a surprising reversal of the way things work in this world and reminds us that our God is no normal God.

There is none like him.

9

FORK IN THE ROAD

As a pastor I get asked lots of questions. Questions about the Bible and marriage, questions about finances and parenting, questions about sex and careers. You name it; I've been asked it.

But there is one question I've been asked more than any other question. It's been asked in the context of a lot of different emotions. Sometimes this question is wrapped in anger, sometimes confusion, and sometimes just pure desperation.

"How can I know God's will for my life?"

Regardless of where you are on your spiritual journey, almost everyone wants to know the peace that comes along with feeling that you're living out God's will for your life. The problem is, I've found that the phrase "God's will" may be one of the most confusing and misused phrases in Christianity today. To one group of people it means one thing, and to another group, it means something completely different.

When we're trying to make a choice to follow the path either of "trusting" God or of "pleasing" God, I think it's important to truly understand what discovering "God's will" means. For in this understanding of God's will, I think it becomes clear which path God intends for us to walk.

When I was in college at Western Kentucky University, I remember having several conversations with my friend Jeremy where he was trying to convince me that it was God's will for him to marry Leesa, a mutual friend of ours.

One of the ways he told me he knew it was God's will was because he had heard a certain song playing, at a certain moment, on a certain radio station.

Leesa never developed any romantic feelings for Jeremy. She actually never gave him the time of day.

Apparently, the song played on the radio wasn't a sign. It wasn't God's will.

A year later this same friend would try to convince me that he didn't know exactly who God wanted him to marry, he knew it was God's will for him to marry someone who "according to worldly standards was unattractive." He thought God was trying to teach him a lesson on humility and vanity and just knew this was God's will. Jeremy was dead set that following God's will for his life required him to choose the path of "pleasing" God. The more difficult the journey, the more confident Jeremy was that he was doing what God wanted.

While he did eventually get married, we lost contact soon after college so I cannot confirm or deny whether his last prompting was actually God's will for his life or not.

A BIG QUESTION MARK

The traditional concept of "God's will" has the ability to cast a huge question mark over our past and future. Understanding its true meaning is fundamental to live the life God has designed for us. Many of us wonder if we've made decisions in our past that were outside of God's will that are wreaking havoc on the present. We wonder if we married the right person, took the right job, moved to the right city, joined the right church, to name a few.

About a month ago Brandi and I took our kids to a farm just outside of Nashville that opens up each fall for people to come visit. They host a fall festival of sorts where you can pick your own pumpkins, visit their petting zoo, and take a hayride. They also have a massive corn maze.

The corn maze is spread out over three acres, and the objective is to begin your journey at one end and navigate your way to the other end. The entire maze is full of places where you have to decide to turn right or left. If you choose correctly, you continue to proceed through the maze. If not, you end up at a dead end that goes nowhere.

Many of us wonder if we've made decisions in our past that were outside of God's will that are wreaking havoc on the present.

I like to think I have an amazing sense of direction, but all three of my boys made it through the maze before I did and they were waiting at the exit to mock me.

I think a lot of us actually think God drops us into this world, which is one big corn maze. As you go through life, you have to make all kinds of decisions.

Do I retire now or do I wait five years?

Should I marry Johnny or Jake?

Should I move to Detroit or San Diego? (For the record I don't think you even need to pray about that one. Let me help you out: it's San Diego.)

Should we keep trying to have our own children or should we adopt?

What do we do? Turn right or left?

We're paralyzed by the fork in the road because we're convinced that if we make the wrong decision, we'll be stuck at a dead end the rest of our life where we have to live out the consequences of getting God's will for our life wrong. Again, this is fueled by a life that's focused on trying to please God. It's like God has this secret plan for our life, but he's not going to tell us what it is. We have to feel our way around in the dark corn maze to figure it out.

This conventional, corn-maze approach to God's will is theologically incorrect and simply not ever what God intended. It's a setup for false guilt and paralyzing doubt. We think of God's will as if there is some sort of specific path we're supposed to follow or a direction we're supposed to go and it's out there somewhere and we're just supposed to keep looking and searching.

I'm not saying God doesn't want you to ask him for wisdom or that he won't help you with direction in your life. I'm certainly not saying God doesn't have a plan for your life.

Look back. You'll see how God's hand has guided you through so many things in life. I just don't believe that God has some secret direction for your life that he expects you to figure out before it happens. He doesn't have a secret path for your life that he's keeping from you.

MOVING FORWARD

When I was a senior in college, I desperately wanted to know God's will for my life. I had worked part-time at a church all the way through college, and so going into ministry felt like a logical next step. I prayed and prayed and prayed but still wasn't sure exactly what I should do next. I was scared to death I was going to miss God's will for my life. I knew ministry was the right next step, but I still had a lot of options.

Should I be a youth pastor? Should I work for an organization like Campus Crusade for Christ or Young Life? Should I do an internship under another senior pastor to learn firsthand how all this church stuff works?

Should I start a church? If I start a church, where would I start a church? Would it be a contemporary church or a traditional church? Would it be a Baptist church or a nondenominational church?

Do I want to go to seminary? Or maybe wait until later?

I prayed until I was exhausted. I was ready to do whatever. Just send me a postcard. Write it in the clouds. Give me something, God. But I would have gotten more clarity with a Magic 8 Ball.

And for a good reason, which I did not understand for many years. God's main purpose for you is not what you do. It's who you become.

Brandi and I have our three boys for the next eighteen years or so. Can you imagine if I told my kids every little thing to do over the next eighteen years? I could tell them exactly what to wear, who to date, what job to take in high school, what college to attend, what subject to major in.

I could do all that if I wanted. And who knows, their life might actually turn out pretty good. But there's one major problem: they would not grow into excellent men.

> God's main purpose for you is not what you do. It's who you become.

We grow, we mature, we transform, and when we have to make choices, we exercise judgment and take responsibility. There is no shortcut in life for this. If I want my children to mature, my will for their life will often be: "You choose."

God knew that I would grow if I had to make choices in ways I would never grow if he just wrote it in the clouds. "God's will" is not a way of escaping the anxiety and responsibility of making decisions.

So as a senior in college, I chose. I chose to start a church, but you know what? I could have chosen any of those ten different options and still been inside God's will.

Many of us today find ourselves at a place in life where we are afraid that we are going to make the wrong decision. We're afraid that we will open the wrong business, move to the wrong city, marry the wrong person, go to the wrong school, or join the wrong church. And we're afraid that when we make that wrong decision, we'll be out of God's will and our life is going to come caving in on us.

The reason so many of us think like this is because over time we have bought into a certain way of thinking as it relates to God's will.

But I believe the vast majority of people start at the wrong place. The teachings of Jesus on the subject of God's will are amazingly easy and simple and surprisingly will rescue you from being focused on the false guilt of your past or the paralyzing doubt of your future.

LIVING OUT THE FUTURE BEFORE IT ARRIVES

Take a look at Matthew 6:25–30, where Jesus encourages us not to worry. He says we don't have to worry about everyday life nor should we because it adds nothing. It changes nothing. Instead he encourages us to seek him, to surrender our concerns and fears to him.

Jesus continues in verses 31–32: "So don't worry about these things, saying, 'What will we eat? What will we drink? What will we wear?' These things dominate the thoughts of unbelievers, but your heavenly Father already knows all your needs."

Jesus could not be clearer in this passage. He doesn't want us to worry about the future. Worrying and fretting and obsessing about the future, even if it is a pseudo-holy worry that is trying to figure out God's will, is not going to add to your life.

I love the way pastor Kevin DeYoung put it in *Just Do Something*: "Anxiety is simply living out the future before it gets here."[1]

Now you want to know God's will for your life. Here you go. Jesus says, "Seek the Kingdom of God above all else, and live righteously, and he will give you everything you need. So don't worry about tomorrow, for tomorrow will bring its own worries. Today's trouble is enough for today" (vv. 33–34).

The decision to be in God's will is not Detroit or San Diego; it's not, do I retire this month or five years from now? It's the daily decision we face to seek God's kingdom or our own kingdom.

The question is not, Should I be a doctor or go into sales? But, Am I loving my neighbor as myself? God's will is your growth in Christlikeness. The apostle Paul reinforced this in 1 Thessalonians: "It is God's will that you should be sanctified. . . . Rejoice always, pray continually, give thanks in all circumstances; for this is God's will for you in Christ Jesus" (1 Thess. 4:3, 5:16–18 NIV).

> God's will is your growth in Christlikeness.

Now some of you may be thinking, *What? I thought God's will would tell me how many kids I should have? I thought it was going to tell me whether to quit my job or not? I thought it was going to tell me whether I should go bowling or play putt-putt Friday night?*

Nope. He says, you know what's worth pondering. You know what's worth your energy and your efforts.

Are you joyful always?

Are you praying continually? In other words, are you living with an awareness of God?

Are you giving thanks in all circumstances?

God's will is about who we are, not where we are. It's about simply trusting him.

A friend of mine who regularly attends AA was telling me about an older lady in his group who will often confess, "You know, I don't know exactly what God's will for me is. I do believe, however, that God's will for me is to do the next best loving thing." She says she doesn't often know what the next right thing is for her, but she can generally tell what the next best loving thing is.

> God's will for you often boils down to doing the next best loving thing.

I love that. God's will for you often boils down to doing the next best loving thing.

Some of you are looking for something a little more concrete, but God's will is your growth in Christlikeness. The moment God's will is figured out with nice, neat lines and definitions, we are no longer dealing with God's will. Sometimes you have to leave what is nailed down, obvious, and secure, and walk into the unknown without any specifics.

And yet God's will is not complicated. Not that following Jesus is always crystal clear in every situation but, as an overarching principle, the will of God for your life is pretty straightforward: love God and love people.

If you do those two things you can be a hairstylist, homemaker, hamburger flipper, historian, handyman, or heart surgeon.

You can live in Nashville, New York, or Nairobi.

You might be at a fork in the road. In front of you might be ten different important decisions that you need to make and ten different paths that you could go. But as you go down whatever path you might choose, love God and love people. This is God's will for you.

Some of you think you've screwed up so bad that you've missed God's will. Not true. You can never fall so far, you can't mess up so bad, that you can't get back in line with God's will for your life.

You might have made some really poor decisions, but God can redeem all of that. Every bit of it.

THIS MOMENT

More often than not, I miss God's will for my life because my mind ricochets between the past and the future.

If you want to learn how to live God's will for your life, you have to learn to be present in the moment, for that's the only way we "seek first the kingdom." And the only way to be present in the moment is to learn how to really trust God with your life.

To live in the moment is a challenging thing to do, in a culture that tempts us with a barrage of distractions. Learning to live in the moment and be fully present is perhaps the most premier skill needed to live the life God has designed for us, which frees us not only from guilt of the past but also from the worry of the future.

> You have to learn to be present in the moment, for that's the only way we "seek first the kingdom."

It is an act of radical trust—trust that God can be encountered at no other time and in no other place than the present moment.

Our challenge is to be here now.

I can't tell you how many times I'm at work and all I can think about is how I wish I was at home with my family. My life seems to be all work, but if I were just at home with them everything would be better.

So then I leave work early to be with them and when I get home, guess what? I'm thinking about work. I start to feel guilty about how there's so much to do and it's all piling up and if I were just back at work crossing some things off of my to-do-list everything would be better.

Sometimes we are never where we are. We bypass the joy of today when we center all our focus on yesterday or tomorrow.

Are you here now, or are you recalling some painful past event? Again, the goal here is not to have no history. The goal is for your past to actually be your past. The goal here is to fully trust God in this moment. To trust in his grace. To trust that you are forgiven. To trust that this very moment, as imperfect as it might be, is actually a gift.

> We bypass the joy of today when we center all our focus on yesterday or tomorrow.

Are you in the present moment, enjoying the beauty right outside your window, the kids in front of you, or the work on your desk; or are you putting off living while you envision some mysterious future paradise over the horizon?

Be here now because this is what Jesus says is best, and we've trusted him with our eternity so we should trust him with our present.

Be here now because your past really is your past. We're learning together that there's nothing we can do about it. It's gone. Forever.

Be here now because your future is unpredictable and uncontrollable. Worrying about it will do nothing for anyone.

Be here now. Not because this moment is perfect, because it most certainly isn't. It may be hard, mean, or even brutal.

But be here now because in the end, life will turn out well because God is good and kind and gracious. He is working mysteriously to redeem us and restore the world to what he intended it to be. All will be well because God is God.

10

SHOWING GRATITUDE

This afternoon I pulled in from work a bit tired and stressed. As I was pulling into my garage, I felt my frustration rise to a new level as once again my kids had left their bicycles right in the middle of my garage where I couldn't pull in. I got out of my truck and slammed the door mumbling under my breath, "How many times do I have to tell those boys to pick up their stuff? Will they ever learn?" As I was walking back to the truck to pull it into the garage, I remember thinking, *Doesn't anyone in this family appreciate how hard I work? Don't they realize that the last thing I want to do after working all day is "work" some more?*

After pulling into the garage, I decided to sit there for a moment and collect my emotions before barging inside. My intentions were to craft a compelling, guilt-drenched speech that would make my family feel sorry for me and hopefully inspire them to seek ways to make my life easier.

But God had a different plan that evening. Sometimes I absolutely hate it when God interrupts my little self-pity parties with his truth and conviction. As I sat there in my truck, I sensed God saying, *Pete, you're missing the whole point here. You're choosing once again to view your life through this selfish lens that robs you of the very blessing of this moment.*

My mind started to go down a completely different track. I thought about the thousands and thousands of couples right now who desperately want to have a child but for some reason can't. I thought about how they would do anything to have to stop and pick up their kids' bikes before they pull into their garage.

God brought to my mind the 3.5 million people in the United States who are homeless. They have no idea where they will lay their head tonight. I, on the other hand, was sitting in a truck that was sitting in my garage. My garage! Not only do I have a home, but I have a home for my car. How crazy blessed am I? All of the sudden, what had been a self-pity rage of sorts was being transformed into a moment of gratitude.

> Gratitude is also one of the most important and most underrated aspects of our walk with God.

I'm discovering a lot about the importance of gratitude these days. It's one of those choices that changes everything. It's been a journey—a journey I'm still very much on. I'm slowly learning how important it is to have gratitude, even in situations and seasons that are challenging and difficult.

Gratitude is a choice. But that choice doesn't come without effort, intentionality, and repetition. Gratitude is also one of the most important and most underrated aspects of our walk with God. It's an important discipline that helps bring healing to our past and hope for our future.

Furthermore, this could impact how I assess my spiritual growth. As I seek to choose to trust God instead of please him, I start asking, In my walk with Jesus, am I becoming a more grateful person or am I becoming more and more of a grumbler?

What's interesting is that when we choose to be more grateful in our lives, we're also learning to trust God more. In fact, gratefulness is the leading quality of someone who chooses to trust God over pleasing him, as we've been discussing.

It's striking how many times in Scripture we are exhorted to give thanks. The psalmist told us, "I will praise God's name in song and glorify him with thanksgiving. This will please the LORD more than an ox, more than a bull with its horns and hooves" (Ps. 69:30–31 NIV) and "Enter his gates with thanksgiving and his courts with praise; give thanks to him and praise his name" (Ps. 100:4 NIV). The apostle Paul told the Colossians, "Whatever you do, whether in word or deed, do it all in the name of the Lord Jesus, giving thanks to God the Father through him" (Col. 3:17 NIV).

It's important to note that gratitude is not just for people whose lives are going exactly the way they hoped. This is where the choice to trust God rather than please him can get difficult. Choosing gratitude in difficult circumstances is not easy, but it is possible. Remember what the apostle Paul said? "Rejoice always, pray continually, give thanks in all circumstances" (1 Thess. 5:16–18 NIV).

Always? Continually? In all circumstances? Is that even possible—in good and bad, joy and sorrow, success and failure, reward and rejection?

According to Henri Nouwen in *Bread for the Journey*, it is: "Still, we are only grateful people when we can say thank you to all that has brought us to the present moment. As long as we keep dividing our lives between events and people we would like to remember and those we would rather forget, we cannot claim the fullness of our beings as a gift of God to be grateful for. Let's not be afraid to look at everything that has brought us to where we are now and trust that we will soon see in it the guiding hand of a loving God."[1]

An important key to not becoming overwhelmed by what is going on around us or even what has happened in our past is looking for evidences of God's hand at work in the midst of the turmoil and being "simply overwhelmed with thankfulness to him."

Below are a few observations regarding gratitude.

1. GRATITUDE IS SILENCED BY ASSUMPTIONS.

There's a game that has been played for generations and generations with small kids. The game has a plethora of names, but the point is always the same: Who can stay quiet the longest? Wise parents all over the world have learned to play this game at strategic times on long road trips when they're frantically searching for a moment of peace.

But gratitude is not a quiet game. In fact, quiet gratitude isn't much use to anyone.

Many of us have gratitude in our hearts that just simply never gets expressed for one reason or another. Often we just assume the person we feel grateful for must already know how we feel. As long as assumptions are present, ingratitude finds all the oxygen it needs to thrive.

> As long as assumptions are present, ingratitude finds all the oxygen it needs to thrive.

I remember several years ago my wife, Brandi, was in a stressful season of mothering. Looking back I don't think I realized just how stressed she was. At the time our boys were five, three, and one. One particular evening we had put all the boys to bed and come downstairs to watch some TV and unwind. For some reason as soon as we sat down I felt prompted to look her in the eyes and just tell her how grateful I was for the incredible job she was doing with our boys. Before I could even finish the complete thought, huge tears started streaming down her face.

She said, "You have no idea how much that means to me. I have so many doubts, I'm so tired, and I just feel like a complete loser." My simple words of gratitude to her filled her with confidence, hope, and a whole new energy.

When it comes to gratitude, you need to say it and show it. If you're really grateful, it will show up in your life.

Stop assuming your spouse knows you're thankful for them. When is the last time you said, "Thank you for doing the dishes" or "For letting me stay at home with the kids" or "For being such a great parent"?

Stop assuming your boss knows how grateful you are for how she invests in you.

Stop assuming your community group leader knows how grateful you are for them opening up their house each week.

Stop assuming your friends know how thankful you are for them listening to you when you're having a bad day.

Stop assuming God knows how thankful you are for sunsets, second chances, and spiritual gifts.

Gratitude is never invisible or silent. Maybe you need to pick up the phone and have a much-needed conversation. Or maybe you need to send a card or an e-mail. Do it now—not tomorrow or next week. Right now.

Who's one person who needs to hear, "I'm thankful for you"?

2. GRATITUDE BEGINS WHERE YOUR SENSE OF ENTITLEMENT ENDS.

As I write this I'm sitting in a cabin out in the middle of nowhere. I'm a long drive from any kind of real civilization. The cell phone coverage out in these parts is a bit sketchy as you might imagine.

A few times today I have wanted to download my e-mail and have been unable to do so. I've found myself getting quite frustrated and complaining about my "stupid, incompetent phone."

But think about it. It's amazing I have any kind of cell service at all out here. It's amazing that I have a phone that can even get e-mail on it. On top of that, most of the time it tells me what the weather is, hosts a billion games I love to play, has a personal assistant that gives me directions, and helps me find restaurants. And this is all done on my phone.

As a kid we had what was called a rotary phone. In case you're not familiar with a rotary phone, it did not check the weather or receive e-mail. You had to stick your finger in the dial and rotate it around. If you grew up with this type of phone, you'll remember just how long it took to even dial a number. Phone numbers with zeros in it were pure torture.

> The higher our sense of entitlement, the lower our sense of gratitude.

I'm learning we can't be grateful for something we feel entitled to, even if it's as simple as a phone or other technology.

This past fall I was in an extremely busy season. I was out of town speaking a lot during the week and then flying back to speak at my church most Sundays. I had simply overcommitted myself and was running on empty. I found myself complaining about all the places I was having to travel to. Toward the end of this long run, God once again convicted me.

There was once a time in my life that I begged God to let me make a difference with my one and only life. I begged him for opportunities to use my gifts. But now what I used to "get to do," today I often say I've "got to do."

The higher our sense of entitlement, the lower our sense of gratitude.

What do you feel entitled to in your life? Your job? Your spouse? Your car? Your kids? Food on your table? Pleasant weather?

Here's what I know: Whatever you feel entitled to, you won't be grateful for. Sometimes we have the tendency to start to think that the good things in our life happen because we deserve them. My family. My house. My career.

The apostle Paul knew about the dangers of entitlement and gave Timothy advice on how to keep it in check: "Command those who are rich in this present world not to be arrogant nor to put their hope in wealth, which is so uncertain, but to put their hope in God, who richly provides us with everything for our enjoyment" (1 Tim. 6:17 NIV).

Everything we have is the direct result of the goodness of God. What does any of us possess that doesn't come down from him? And if we start to focus too much on the gifts, we forget the giver.

Focusing on the gifts will make you want more; focusing on the giver makes you grateful.

In *The Shattered Lantern*, Ronald Rolheiser wrote, "The original sin of Adam and Eve, the prototype of all sin, is presented as a failure to be receptive and grateful."[2] Think about it for a second: God creates Adam and Eve and places them in the garden where they are surrounded by unmistakable beauty and all the goodness of life. They are experiencing the fullness of life, the way it was intended to be, and are promised it will continue under one condition: just don't eat the fruit of a certain tree. We all know that, however, they would eventually fail to receive life as a gift and instead try to seize it as if it were owed to them.

When I think of my own life and the sin that often creeps in, it usually begins with my failure to see life as a gift—my lust, pride, anger, lack of forgiveness. It's the overflow of a heart that begins to believe that something is "owed" to me, and it keeps me from being fully present and appreciative of what I have. I have to remind myself often that if God never gives me one more thing, I still owe him everything, my entire life.

If he doesn't breathe out, we don't breathe in. He thought us into existence. If we view our life, our circumstances, our relationships, and yes, even our hardships and challenges as gifts, how different would our lives be?

3. GRATITUDE IS MOST OFTEN ABOUT PERSPECTIVE.

A while back someone had purchased a kite and given it to my youngest son as a gift. It sat in his room for weeks as he would on a regular basis ask me to get it out and fly it. I wanted to fly the kite, but our yard is full of trees and I knew it would get caught in one. I was waiting for a time to take him to the park, but things kept getting in the way.

Finally one day before I was getting ready to go to the airport he asked me again if I would fly it with him. I couldn't turn him down, so I warned him again it would more than likely get stuck in a tree but agreed to run out there with him for a few minutes.

We got the kite up in the air with no problems. Brewer was having a blast, but as I feared after about ten minutes it predictably got stuck in the tree. He just stood there staring at the motionless kite lodged in between several branches.

> Grateful people can find a blessing in almost any situation.

As we walked inside I was afraid he was going to be absolutely crushed. Instead he grabbed my hand as we bounced up the stairs and said, "Dad, that was the best time ever!" I realized that, from his perspective, flying a kite and getting it stuck in the tree was better than not flying a kite at all.

Grateful people can find a blessing in almost any situation. And the opposite is also true. Negative people can find a burden or create a burden in almost any situation.

A couple of weeks ago I was in Toronto, Canada, to speak at a Promise Keepers conference. The driver who picked me up from the airport was a middle-aged man named Lucas who was from the Philippines. En route to the arena, we were talking about life and family. He had four children (all of them almost out of the house) but was the youngest of eleven brothers and sisters. He spoke a briefly about how he made it to Toronto and how much he loved living in Canada.

We were sitting in Toronto traffic trying to get to the event I was speaking at. As we got closer to the bottleneck, I realized it was a construction project. During the middle of our small talk I couldn't help but think, *Stupid traffic. Stupid construction. Will they ever finish all these projects?* As we drove through the construction, however, Lucas chimed in with. "Sure is wonderful that the government here has the resources to fix up the roads like this. In the Philippines we didn't have these kind of resources and the roads are virtually impassable throughout most of the country."

Gratitude is based on not how good your situation is but how good you see your situation to be. That's why someone with half of what you have can be so much more thankful than you.

People who have chosen to make gratitude their mind-set and lifestyle can view anything through the eyes of thankfulness. The whole world looks different when we do. And a grateful man or woman will be a breath of fresh air in a world contaminated by bitterness, cynicism, and discontentment. When you choose gratitude, not only do you choose to let hope into your own life, but you let hope in for countless others.

WHAT DO YOU SAY?

The grateful heart is not developed in a single moment; it is the result of a thousand choices. It's a repetitive choice that transforms our hearts and becomes a part of us over time. And I've found that the more we choose gratitude in the present, the less power a painful past has over us.

One of the first word combinations children of all languages are taught is "Thank you." I remember my parents prompting me regularly with, "What do you say?" to get me to say those two words. Any time they asked me, "What do you say?" I knew the appropriate response was, "Thank you."

> The grateful heart is not developed in a single moment; it is the result of a thousand choices.

So tomorrow morning when God opens your eyes, what do you say?

Next time you laugh so hard your face hurts, what do you say?

When you're so in love that you can't even eat, what do you say?

When you look out the window and see God's beautiful creation, what do you say?

Thank you for the gift of loving and being loved.

Thank you for the rainbow after a summer storm.

Thank you for the smile on the face of a little child.

How about when you open the Bible and read that God loves you and that he has given you the gift of sight, sound, and touch; the gift of the church; and most important, the gift of his Son, Jesus, who paid the price that you should have paid so that you could have eternal life with him? When you read that God has given you gift after gift after gift, what do you say?

Thank you.

Because all is grace.

CHOICE FOUR:

CHOOSING TO FREE PEOPLE RATHER THAN HURT THEM

11

BREATHE GRACE

Have you ever had someone you count on make a promise and then break it?

How about a close friend who takes a deep secret that you shared in confidence and tells somebody else?

Maybe you had someone who was entrusted to care for you but instead hurt you in one of the deepest ways imaginable by abusing you physically or sexually?

A business partner gains your trust and then exploits it?

How about an ex-spouse who took the love you had for one another and ruined it by cheating on you?

If you live long enough, chances are you'll be hurt or betrayed by someone. Betrayal is not just being hurt by somebody; it's being hurt by someone you thought you could count on. Betrayal is always a violation of trust and a breaking of a promise. It comes at the hand of a friend, spouse, coworker, or boss. And like a sucker punch, it always comes as a shock.

> Betrayal is not just being hurt by somebody; it's being hurt by someone you thought you could count on.

The crippling reality is that if we don't do something with that hurt or betrayal, it will assault us every time it comes to our mind. It will keep us prisoner of our past because that hurt will impact everything we touch—whether it's sleeping, traveling, dreaming, or parenting.

Some of you have somehow convinced yourself that you can manage the hurt from your past without offering forgiveness. In fact, maybe you even tell yourself that you can hardly remember the pain. But unfortunately, the pains we dare not remember are often the most dangerous pains of all. We fear these particular hurts so much that we stuff them deep into our heart and past. But they always come back. Usually disguised, but they always come back.

Sometimes you don't forgive someone for their sake; you do it for your own freedom.

In *Forgive and Forget*, theologian Lewis Smedes wrote, "Our hate does not even have the decency to die when those we hate die—for it is a parasite sucking our blood, not theirs."[1]

You may be completely justified for the bitterness you have. You may have every right to not forgive certain people in your life. But you need to know bitterness contaminates everything. It spreads far and wide and deep. Bitterness doesn't isolate to the source of bitterness; it spreads to all of your relationships. And left unchecked, it will ruin everything that is important to you.

Which is why sometimes you don't forgive someone for their sake; you do it for your own freedom.

SLIPPERY SLOPE

I met Gerry and his wife, Brenda, several years ago at church. Gerry is quite a bit older than I am, but there was a certain kind of peace this man radiated that made me want to get to know him better.

I took them to lunch one day to hear their story and hung on to his every word over the next hour and a half. Gerry knew Brenda was the one for him the moment they met.

"We had several college classes together and although she didn't even seem to be aware that I was alive, I made it my whole goal to get on her radar. Eventually I succeeded and actually talked that woman into marrying me. How lucky am I?" he said as he chuckled.

As soon as they were married, friends and relatives started asking when they were going to start a family. A year and a half into their marriage they decided to abandon contraception. As Gerry put it, "I remember how scared and yet excited we were at the same time, and Brenda immediately went into baby mode. We were shopping for baby clothes—for some reason we always thought it was going to be a little boy—looking at cribs, debating our favorite names, and arguing over what color we would paint the nursery. We were quite confident Brenda would get pregnant quickly."

Gerry and Brenda, like so many other couples, were simply not prepared for the long battle they had ahead of them. Months and months would pass, and every single time Brenda got her period, she would burst into tears.

Over the next four years, they would spend every ounce of hope and their entire financial savings trying procedure after procedure in a desperate series of attempts to get pregnant. They had prayed about adoption but for some reason or another the door never opened for them.

After giving up on the idea that Brenda would ever be able to get pregnant, out of the blue, she started to show symptoms that she might in fact be pregnant. "I put off buying a pregnancy test for weeks. It had been almost four years since I had bought my last pregnancy test and I remember the deep disappointment every time I looked at that stupid test and saw that it was negative," Brenda said.

But on March 14, 1984, despite all the odds, Gerry and Brenda had a baby girl and named her Annie, which meant "blessed by grace." They freely admit that Annie was a pretty spoiled child as they spent the next eighteen years showering her with love and attention. Gerry said, "You know, I felt like every day that I looked into her eyes was another reminder of the grace of God. She was such a gift to us and we never forgot that. We celebrated her life often."

So you can imagine how heartbroken they were when during Annie's freshman year of college, her life began to unravel. Despite their continuous warnings to Annie and their frequent surprise visits they made over the course of the year, Annie dropped out of college and was living with some friends over two hundred miles away from home.

"We were absolutely crushed," Brenda recalled. "We were already struggling with allowing our daughter to move away for college and how to do life without the one thing it seemed like our life had been built around. Almost from the time we were married, we were either praying we could have a baby or taking care of that baby."

Eventually Gerry and Brenda discovered that their daughter's problems were being fueled by a heavy drug addiction. "This was the darkest time of our life," Gerry said. "The only thing worse than the seven years of waiting in the dark for our dream to be achieved was now watching this dream self-destruct and not being able to do a thing about it."

During her freshman year of college, Annie had gotten mixed up with the wrong group of people, mainly, a guy named Kyle. He introduced her to drugs, and the rest was downhill from there. She lived with Kyle in a drug-induced stupor for the next two years. There were weeks they would disappear and nobody would know where they were or hear from them. Brenda and Gerry spent many nights crying and praying, fearing that she was dead in some heroin house.

As Gerry recalled, "It was crushing our hearts and our marriage. I had to blame someone, so I blamed this guy Kyle. I had tried several times to drive up to Indiana to get her, to rescue her, but she would never come with me. I was convinced that Kyle was manipulating her. I was convinced that if it wasn't for him my daughter would not be doing drugs and not be in the shape she was."

In one of his final attempts to rescue Annie, he drove four hours and literally broke down the door to the little shack they were living in. He tried dragging her out, but Kyle hit him over the head with a lamp, so Gerry headed back home.

Gerry was fueled with anger for Kyle. "For the first time in my life, I allowed my hatred to take me to a dark place. I began daydreaming about how I could kill Kyle. I thought about how I would do it and how I would cover it up. I convinced myself it was the only thing I could do to get my daughter back. I planted a seed of hate in my heart that night, and the root of bitterness began to grow. It was fertilized daily by my thoughts of getting rid of Kyle. I was on a slippery slope."

ABSORBING THE DEBT

Hate is our natural response to any deep and unfair pain. It's an instinctive backlash against anyone who wounds us wrongly. Nobody wants to admit they hate someone, because it makes us feel cruel and malicious.

Maybe you wish your ex-husband would have some kind of tragedy in his life that would leave him miserably unhappy with his new wife.

Maybe you wish the coworker who embarrassed you in front of everyone would get fired.

Hate makes you want to see them hurt in the same way they made you hurt. It makes you dream about evening the score.

One day, Jesus was trying to make a point about forgiveness and so he told a story. Generally, when Jesus wanted to make a life-changing point he would do it via a simple story. This one was about a king who was settling debts with his servants. "As he began the settlement, a man who owed him ten thousand talents was brought to him. Since he was not able to pay, the master ordered that he and his wife and his children and all that he had be sold to repay the debt. The servant fell on his knees before him. 'Be patient with me,' he begged, 'and I will pay back everything.' The servant's master took pity on him, canceled the debt and let him go" (Matt. 18:24–27 NIV).

> Hate is our natural response to any deep and unfair pain.

Imagine for a moment the fear and utter sense of humiliation this servant must feel. He is going to be either thrown in jail or sold into slavery. And not just him, but also his whole family would be sold into slavery. And not just for this generation, but for generations to come. A slave was worth maybe two thousand dollars. So the sale of his whole family into slavery would not pay for even one-tenth of one percent of the debt. Ten thousand talents was a massive debt. One single talent is worth about sixteen years of wages. He owes upward of 160,000 years of wages, which meant he is facing slavery for him, his wife, his children, and his descendants for generations and generations to come. For reasons probably no one understands, the master says, "You're not going to be a slave. You're not going to lose your family. You may keep what you owe. You are set free."

When the owner forgives the debt, the debt doesn't just disappear. The owner absorbs it and takes the loss. It costs the owner the equivalent of hundreds of millions of dollars when he forgives his servant. This is a huge debt that's forgiven.

The master in this story, of course, represents God. The other main character in this story, the servant, is you and me. Jesus said that we have accumulated a moral debt before a just and holy God and have been adding to it for years, every time we were less than loving to another person, every time we had a lustful thought or judgmental attitude, every time we gossiped, we were adding to our debt at a rapid pace.

Jesus was saying that God looked at you, looked at me, and was moved with compassion. He then sent his Son, Jesus, to die on a cross the death that, by all rights, I should have died because of my sinfulness. The death that you should have died. The death that we deserved to die, he died instead on the cross.

The Bible says that on the cross Jesus paid our debt and absorbed the loss so that we could be free. The place that ultimately expresses God's forgiveness is the cross.

THE WAY OF LOVE OVER HATE

In the story Jesus was telling, the servant is off the hook. He owes his life, his freedom, his family, his possessions, everything to the grace of his master. He doesn't have to repay a cent. So everybody listening to this story wanted to know, how was this guy going to respond? What will his life look like in the second chapter?

Jesus continued, "But when that servant went out, he found one of his fellow servants who owed him a hundred denarii. He grabbed him and began to choke him. 'Pay back what you owe me!' he demanded. His fellow servant fell to his knees and begged him, 'Be patient with me, and I will pay you back.' But he refused.

Instead, he went off and had the man thrown into prison until he could pay the debt" (Matt. 18:28–30 NIV).

And this is the same servant who was just forgiven everything, who was completely set free. He thinks to himself, "I'm not going to make the same mistake the master made with me. I'm not going to get stuck with it," and he won't forgive the debt. He essentially says in his heart, "I'm going to make you pay."

It's normal for human beings to want to retaliate. When someone pushes us, it's instinctive to want to push back. When someone raises their voice at us, we want to yell back a little louder. When someone hurts us, we want to see them get hurt back.

I felt this as Gerry was telling me his story. Of course, he was furious with his daughter's boyfriend. He felt as if this guy was hurting one of the most precious things to him. It was natural for him to want to retaliate, to get even. As Gerry was telling me his story, it never once crossed my mind that his anger, his vengeance, his hate, was unjustified.

Here's the truth about forgiveness, though: authentic forgiveness is never cheap. When we get hurt and the hurt is deep and the hurt is unfair, we want the other person to get hurt back. We want them to know the pain that they've inflicted on us. We want them to pay. I know what that feels like. You do too. Especially those of you who have been hurt in unjust, deeply unfair ways. We just want the other person to pay. It's human nature.

In essence, someone has run up a moral debt with you, and you know it to the penny. You're thinking, *Yeah, but if I forgive him, I know what that means. It means I'm going to have to swallow the debt. I'll have to pay the cost. And the cost is not making them hurt back, not getting even, letting it go.*

Understanding how God has received us is the only place we'll ever get the resources to receive others when they've sinned against us. The only way we'll be able to forgive others when they wrong us is understanding that when we sin against God, when we run as far away from him as we can, when we return, he receives us. When we get that, when that moves from our head to our heart, we understand that we can't do anything but forgive people when they wrong us. We can't help but begin to let go of the hate that has us barricaded in the past.

As we forgive people, we gradually begin to see them differently. Our hate

> As we forgive people, we gradually begin to see them differently.

blinds us, keeping us from seeing them apart from what they've done to us. But forgiveness allows us to see deeper into them.

They are people who hurt us; however, this is not what is most true of them.

They were broken human beings before they hurt us, and they are broken human beings after they hurt us.

They are hurting, needy, and weak before they hurt us, and they are hurting, needy, and weak after they hurt us.

I'm not saying it becomes easy, but when you understand how you have wronged God and that you have been a messed-up person who has only sinned against him your entire life and yet he's received you through the death of his Son, you are compelled to forgive other people. My understanding of God's forgiving me despite me enables me to forgive others despite others. And while this act of forgiveness may not erase your past hurt, it does erase the power it has over you. It all allows your past to truly become just that—your past.

It is impossible to truly forgive others in our own strength, especially when they have hurt us deeply or betrayed our trust. We can try not to think about what they did or stuff our feelings deep inside and put on a false smile when we see them. But unless our heart is cleansed and changed by God, the memories and the feelings will still be lurking in the background, poisoning our thoughts and words, and preventing the rebuilding of trust and relationship. There is only one way to overcome these barriers, and that is to admit that we cannot forgive in our own strength and that we desperately need God to come in and change our heart. Once we have let hope in and are inhaling God's grace, only then are we able to help others by offering them hope and grace.

> You can't breathe out what you haven't breathed in.

Flight attendants are very familiar with this concept. Before every flight, they explain how in case of an emergency, oxygen bags will open up and how passengers must secure their own mask before assisting others. Flight attendants understand that if passengers attempt to help others first, they could be in danger of not only losing oxygen themselves if there's a loss of cabin pressure but also not being able to continue assisting others. Passengers, on the other hand, who are breathing the oxygen first are able to help as many others as they can reach.

You can't breathe out what you haven't breathed in. Breathing grace totally hinges on your moment-to-moment dependency on God. We have to find ways to continually "breathe in" God's grace.

I think it's essentially impossible to really forgive someone if we don't trust God for the supernatural strength. It's just not in most of us. Unless we understand how the Father, through Jesus Christ's death and resurrection, has received us, I don't know where else we get the resources to begin the journey of forgiveness.

IT TAKES TIME

Years ago I left a job and community I loved, to work with someone I trusted. Unfortunately, on the first day of the job, I started to see some inconsistencies between the way he acted in public and the way he acted behind closed doors. He had huge mood swings that would take him from acting as giddy as a child to instantaneously being fueled with rage. He had a horrible habit of verbally abusing those closest to him.

Over time I observed and experienced other issues that kept me from—in good conscious—continuing to work for this man. The day I went into his office to tell him I was resigning, he began demeaning me by calling me "immature and careless" and went as far as saying, "Your father failed because he raised a quitter."

As I walked out of his office that day, I tasted a little hate toward that man. He hurt me deeply. For months when I found myself doubting a decision, I would recall his malicious words, which would make me doubt myself further. At the same time it also made me madder and madder at how he had hurt me.

A year later, seeing my hurt and bitterness toward him exhibit itself in many different ways in my life, I decided that I really wanted to get rid of my hate. I started praying daily for God to allow me to release this man. I came to the realization that while I couldn't control what had happened to me, I could control what happens within me.

Ironically, after praying that for about two weeks, I ran into him one day at lunch. I knew what I had to do. I needed to approach him and reach deep into my heart to extend a kindness to him that I really didn't have.

To this day I believe God prodded me out of my seat to go approach him, because as I walked across the floor of that restaurant, I remember thinking the whole way, *What are you doing? What are you going to say?*

I approached my former employer with a desire to make this right. I extended my right hand out to shake his hand. He wasn't alone. In fact, there were four or five staff people with him who I used to work with. It was an odd moment for all of us.

There I stood with my hand out. As the seconds went by (they felt more like hours) with no response from him, the more I started to think that this was a horrible idea. Eventually, he lifted his hand from his side, and instead of shaking mine, he swatted it down, turned, and walked away.

While things that day didn't go as I had hoped, it was still a turning point for me. In fact, over the next couple of months, I found myself attempting to understand why he acted the way he acted. Hurt people, hurt people. I know it's a cliché, but clichés are often true. It doesn't excuse what they've done in any way. I just find it amazing how a little understanding makes forgiving a lot easier.

> Sometimes forgiveness takes time. Sometimes it takes so long you actually can't remember the moment you did it.

Sometimes forgiveness takes time. Sometimes it takes so long you actually can't remember the moment you did it. You just kind of wake up one day, and when you think of that person, you're surprised to discover that you don't hate them near as much. You realize you've actually started to forgive them without even consciously making a decision to.

I remember several years later I ran into my former employer again. He was in a much better place and this time he actually approached me. We never became great friends or even had a deep heart-to-heart talk about the past, but we did come to an unstated mutual agreement that we were letting go of what had happened between us.

I had finally let go of my desire for an even score. Forgiveness for me didn't come in a single decision. It came in bits and pieces with a greeting here and an unplanned conversation there. I kind of stumbled into it.

Forgiveness looked similar for my friend Gerry as well. After about two years Annie, whom he thought he would never have a relationship with again, moved back home. The abusive relationship she had with Kyle was finally over. But even though he had his daughter back, his hatred for Kyle continued to rage.

At our lunch, Gerry said, "Pete, one day I woke up and knew I had to let this anger go. It was damaging my ability to love anyone. I had become a bitter, wound-up, short-tempered man, because my vengeance was slowly poisoning me. It took me a while, but day by day I began to let the hurt go. I continually reflected on the love and forgiveness of Jesus and asked God to fill me with what he had already extended to me."

The big moment for Gerry came just over two years ago when one day he did the unthinkable. "I asked my daughter if Kyle still worked at the same plant he had for years. She assured me that as far as she knew he was. So that morning, not able to take it anymore, I started the four-hour drive to track him down. It occurred to me on my way up there that I really didn't know what I was going to say if I got the chance to talk to him."

When Gerry reached there, he asked to speak with Kyle. "I didn't know whether to be excited or scared. I guess I was a little of both. Just a few minutes later there he was standing before me. It had been six years since I had seen him last, but hardly a day had gone by that I hadn't brought his face to mind."

Gerry cut right to the chase. "Kyle, I'm here to say that I'm sorry. I've held a lot of anger toward you over the years for what I felt you had done to Annie and I want you to know I'm sorry."

"How is Annie?" Kyle asked.

"She's fine," Gerry said. "She's clean and working hard. We're very proud of her."

Kyle stood there for a minute before responding. "That's good to hear. Listen, I appreciate you driving all this way to say what you said. I'm sorry too, man. I've made a lot of mistakes in my own life."

"Haven't we all?" Gerry then extended his hand to shake Kyle's.

"Man, that's not going to cut it after all we've been through," Kyle said as he leaned forward to give Gerry a hug.

As Gerry stood there in the lobby of this plant embracing Kyle, he felt a peace come over him that he hadn't felt in years.

Minutes later he was back in the car headed home. As Gerry explained, "The last time I was driving this direction on this road, I was contemplating killing a man because I was filled with so much rage and hate toward him. This time I was beginning to be filled with love toward the same man, whom I had just finished embracing. Never forget how powerful of a miracle forgiveness is."

FORGIVENESS IS NOT CONDONING

In recent years I've spent a lot of time with people who desperately want to experience the healing that comes along with forgiving someone. And with each one of them, generally there is one of three hurdles that seem to stand in the way of forgiveness.

The first hurdle is the idea that forgiving is the same as condoning. *Forgiving is not condoning.* It does not mean that you condone what someone did that was wrong. It does not mean that you excuse what someone did. Forgiveness is not the same thing as excusing someone. It does not mean that you decide you will tolerate injustice. Injustice needs to be fought at every turn.

Forgiveness is the opposite of excusing. The fact that forgiveness is needed and granted indicates that what someone did was wrong and inexcusable. Forgiveness says, "We both know that what you did was wrong and without excuse. But since God has forgiven me, I forgive you." Because forgiveness deals honestly with sin, it brings a freedom that no amount of excusing or condoning could ever hope to provide.

The second hurdle is the idea that forgiving means you always reconcile with the other person. *Forgiving is not reconciling.* Sometimes you cannot reconcile. Remember what the apostle Paul said: "If it is possible, as far as it depends on you, live at peace with everyone" (Rom. 12:18 NIV). Note the phrase "If it is possible," meaning sometimes it's just not possible. If the other person is not willing to acknowledge their part, if they are not willing to confess and repent when they have wronged you, then you cannot reconcile. You cannot build a relationship safely unless it's built on truth. Without truth, there's no trust. Without trust, you have no relationship.

> You cannot build a relationship safely unless it's built on truth.

The third hurdle is that people often confuse forgiveness and forgetting. *Forgiving is not the same as forgetting.* In fact, we need to forgive precisely because we have not forgotten what someone did. Forgetting is a passive process in which a matter fades from memory merely with the passing of time. Forgiving is an active process; it involves a conscious choice and a deliberate course of action.

The writer of Isaiah tells us that God "remembers your sins no more" (43:25 NIV). He's not saying he can't remember our sins; rather, he's saying he will not remember them. When he forgives us, he chooses not to mention, recount, or think about our sins ever again.

Similarly, when we forgive, we must draw on God's grace and consciously decide not to think or talk about what others have done to hurt us. This may require a lot of effort, especially when an offense is still fresh in mind. Fortunately, when we decide to forgive someone and stop dwelling on an offense, painful memories usually begin to fade.

Again, forgiveness doesn't mean you forget, excuse, tolerate, or overlook; rather, it means you choose the way of love over hate, letting go of your right to hurt them back.

Forgiving someone means knowing full well that the offense was inappropriate, improper, or out-and-out wrong—and then deciding to relinquish your feelings of being entitled to make the guilty person pay.

You can always forgive, because what it means to forgive someone is to let go of your desire to see them hurt. You let it go. This takes time because it's a process.

AN ACT OF TRUST

With forgiveness there is a vertical transaction and a horizontal transaction. This is where we're learning to trust God, because we start with this vertical transaction. In an act of trust, we hand over the responsibility of what to do next to God. We fully acknowledge the wrong done to us, and we place both the act and the consequences into his hands.

> With forgiveness there is a vertical transaction and a horizontal transaction.

When someone hurts us, there are consequences. We're going to live with the consequences whether we want to or not. Our only choice is whether we will do so in the bitterness of unforgiveness or the freedom of forgiveness.

Forgiveness is me giving up the right to hurt you for hurting me. Instead of hurting you for hurting me, I make a conscious choice to free you despite hurting me.

While hurt people will hurt people, free people will free people.

And when someone hurts us, Jesus stands with us. He stands in us. His word to us is that he hopes we'll forgive this person, this offense in the same way he forgave us. That we'll trust him to heal us, restore us, and free us from the hurt.

Some of you may be carrying this burden around. Put it down today. Because if you don't, it'll ruin you. It costs a lot to forgive, but to not forgive costs you even more—your heart. Don't forgive and you will become chained to your anger and resentment. Don't forgive and bit by bit all the joy will get choked out of you. Don't forgive and you won't be able to trust again. Don't forgive and the bitterness will crowd the compassion out of your heart, slowly, utterly, forever.

I long for you to experience this miracle of extending forgiveness. It's a miracle because even though we might still have the memory, forgiveness allows us to assert our God-given power to let go. When our past can no longer control or destroy us, it becomes a collection of experiences that deepen the wisdom of our heart. It brings us to a place of empathy and compassion for others. Whether or not we forget, forgiveness undeniably acts as a healing balm to the memories we carry.

I believe the Bible teaches that the only power to forgive lies in the experience of being forgiven. As the apostle Paul wrote, "Instead, be kind to each other, tenderhearted, forgiving one another, just as God through Christ has forgiven you" (Eph.4:32).

The only thing that gives us fallen, messed-up people the power to extend grace to anyone is the experience of being forgiven by a holy God. No clever principles or simple steps. Just the cross.

The cross is the place where we see the ultimate expression of the heart of God. The cross is God's ultimate tool against the anger and hostility, hurt and hate that would otherwise destroy the human race.

Now you choose:

Vengeance or mercy?

Prison or freedom?

Hatred or grace?

Death or life?

We are never so free as when we reach back into our past and forgive a person who caused us pain. Inhale grace and then breathe it back out again, choosing to bless someone instead of cursing yourself. After all, God gave you the cross.

12

OVERCOMING FEAR

What's your worst fear? A fear of public failure, unemployment, or heights? The fear that you'll never find the right spouse or be completely healthy again? The fear of being trapped, abandoned, or forgotten?

One of the things I'm praying is that as you read this book, as you begin to let hope in, it will give you the needed strength to face down the obstacles that stand between you and your better self, today and your better tomorrow.

According to Max Lucado in his book *Fearless*, Jesus issues 125 commands or imperatives. Of those 125, twenty-one of them have to do with this topic of fear and encourage us to "not be afraid" or "not fear" or "have courage" or "take heart." The second most common command, to love God and neighbor, appears only eight times.

Quantity in Scripture doesn't always equal importance, but it's safe to assume that Jesus takes our fears quite seriously. The one statement he made more than any other was, "Don't be afraid." He said it fifteen times in the four Gospels.

When Jairus thought his daughter was lost forever, Jesus said to him, "Don't be afraid; just believe, and she will be healed" (Luke 8:50 NIV).

When the disciples saw Jesus walking to them on water and thought he was someone who might harm them, he immediately said to them: "Take courage! It is I. Don't be afraid" (Matt 14:27 NIV).

When the disciples were worried about the future and full of doubt, Jesus encouraged them by saying, "Peace I leave with you; my peace I give you. I do not give to you as the world gives. Do not let your hearts be troubled and do not be afraid" (John 14:27 NIV).

One of the fears I think most of us develop is a fear of the unknown.

Psychologists tell us we were all born with two fears: the fear of falling and the fear of loud noises. I am not sure how much truth there is to that, but it makes sense to me. One of the next fears I think most of us develop is a fear of the unknown. In fact, for some of you, the fear of the unknown is what drives you to keep visiting your past.

There's a great example of this dynamic found in the Old Testament. God had freed his people, the Israelites, from over four hundred years of slavery. Almost from the moment they were free and on the journey to the land, the life that God had for them, they started to complain. They couldn't stand the unknown. It seemed as if God had provided for them at every turn.

When they were trapped, he provided a way out.

When they were lost, he guided them.

When they were hungry, he fed them.

But the unknown was too much. So they cried out for the past. They were willing to forgo their newly found freedom, which required journeying into the unknown, to go back to be slaves where they could at least know what to expect.

Listen to how the author of Exodus put it: "In the desert the whole community grumbled against Moses and Aaron. The Israelites said to them, 'If only we had died by the LORD's hand in Egypt! There we sat around pots of meat and ate all the food we wanted, but you have brought us out into this desert to starve this entire assembly to death'" (16:2–3 NIV).

Want to know why some of you are stuck in your past? Want to know why some of the same painful moments feel as though they're on replay in your life? You choose it.

You've consciously—or maybe subconsciously—made a choice that you would rather stay in the predictable patterns of your past (no matter how painful they might be) than take a risk and venture into the unknown.

John Lennon once said, "The unknown is what it is. And to be frightened of it is what sends everybody scurrying around chasing dreams, illusions, wars, peace, love, hate, all that—it's all illusion. Unknown is what it is. Accept that it's unknown and it's plain sailing."[1]

Not real helpful but partially true.

At our house we have a fenced-in backyard. I believe this is essential when you have three wild boys who love to play outside. Well, let me clarify. They love to play in the dirt. I think if we had a lot of dirt in the house, they would probably be just as happy playing inside.

When they're in the fenced-in backyard, we have a level of comfort as parents. We know they're safe or at least safer than if they were outside the fence.

Inside the fence we can control the variables. We've removed most of the weapons (sticks, rocks). Outside the fence we don't have as much control of the variables.

Inside the fence is known. Outside the fence is unknown.

Now expand this idea to your life. There is inside the fence (the known, the comfortable) and then there is outside the fence (the unknown, the unpredictable).

We all have a fence in our mind. You know about that flutter you get in your stomach, the stutter you get in your speech, the sickening feeling you have when you get close to the edge of familiarity.

Most of us hate that feeling of not knowing what's next.

Most of us hate that feeling of not knowing what's next.

We feel fear daily. For many of us it may be an almost constant companion. Something happens and we immediately imagine that the worst will certainly follow. We then either become passive or overreact. Not only do our minds not drift toward hope, but they actually keep coming up with reasons to fear even more.

The human brain is an amazing thing. Different parts of your brain have different functions. The first part of your brain you use every day to do your thinking, problem solving, and daily work and chores.

The second part is much different. It works on autopilot and could be called a "primitive brain." It takes care of things like your heartbeat, your breathing, and your balance that allows you to walk. But the major function for this primitive brain is to keep you safe. Our brains are literally trained throughout our lives to discern between what is okay and what is dangerous. It keeps us alert for danger and prepared to make quick judgments if there are threats. When we accidently touched the hot stove when we were young, the safety center in our head logged that information and learned.

Over time as our safety center continues to expand, it begins this interpretation that if something is unfamiliar or unknown, it could be dangerous. Only trust the things we know. Now the result of when we get too close to the edge of what's familiar, our brain sends off all the same warning signals and red flags. It sends off the same warnings it would if we absentmindedly got too close to the hot stove. The problem is, of course, that we do not always need that response; there are many false alarms that occur over our lifetime. It's there to protect us, but it can also perpetuate a feeling of fear that, if trusted, will keep us fenced in a safe little area away from opportunity and growth.

And to complicate things further, most of us do not automatically act bravely; we need encouragement. It's as if we need a certain validation of our courage before it can be activated. The encouragement was supposed to begin in childhood, which is exactly why for some of you, your past doesn't remain in your past.

You may have childhood wounds that have been accrued because of your parents failing at granting you that support. What results is an ongoing struggle between the part of us that longs for something new and the part of us that fears so much we always return to the past. Once again we see that our past is not our past. It's wreaking havoc on our present. These layers of fear we picked up as kids do not go away; we just keep piling on new layers on top of them.

Our fears establish the limits of our life.

If we fear heights, we will stay low.

If we fear people, we'll stay alone.

If we fear failure, we simply won't try.

So when many of us encounter circumstances in life that are unplanned, our instinct is to become paralyzed. Even if this unplanned circumstance could lead us to the life God has for us. We allow the fear of the unknown to establish the limits of our life. We can't make decisions, we can't move, we can't grow. And yet this is not God's will for our lives.

This can be a monumental problem. Our minds have often

been trained over time to think fear. To think worst-case scenarios. To desire to stay inside the comfortable, predictable fence. We need to retrain.

The apostle Paul reminds us to "not conform any longer to the pattern of this world, but be transformed by the renewing of your mind. Then you will be able to test and approve what God's will is—his good, pleasing and perfect will" (Rom. 12:2 NIV). There are currently several patterns in our world that we should not conform to, including the pattern of hurry and the pattern of debt. But one of the patterns I see every single day is fear. Scripture tells us to learn to retrain or renew our mind: "Trust in the LORD with all your heart and do not lean on your own understanding" (Prov. 3:5 NASB).

> We can't always trust our own mind, our own understanding, because it's been somewhat trained by the patterns of this world.

It's implied that we can't always trust our own mind, our own understanding, because it's been somewhat trained by the patterns of this world. It's been trained by the past. Don't always trust in the red flag your mind throws. Don't always back away from fear because it's possible that God is calling you to run diametrically opposed to what your mind is warning. The beauty for those who claim to follow Christ is we can trust in something far more reliable than our own mind and understanding.

FASHIONED FOR FAITH

One of Jesus' most brilliant teachings can be found in the book of Matthew. He addresses the worry, fear, and anxiety each one of us tends to experience when going through life. "Do not worry [be anxious] about your life, what you will eat or drink; or about your body, what you will wear. Is not life more important than food, and the body more important than clothes?" (6:25 NIV).

Remember, Jesus is specifically addressing basic physical needs here, but I think it has a wider application. Jesus isn't saying we should never be concerned about the fact we just lost our job, the economy is tanking, our marriage is unraveling, or our kids are straying. Instead he's saying he wants to give you a different perspective for a moment.

As a pastor I've had quite a few opportunities to walk with people who have been only days from passing from this life. The similarity in those conversations is almost uncanny as they almost always talk about how they "get it." They understand they've spent too much of their lives worrying and fearing things that just weren't worth it. They usually crave to have those moments in life back.

Just last week I did a funeral for a mother of three young children who was killed in a tragic car accident. She was married. At her memorial service, person after person got up talking about how her sudden death was such a wake-up call for them. Dozens of people got up to speak and almost every one of them had a similar message: I had forgotten what was really important in life.

So Jesus is not saying we shouldn't be concerned; rather, he's saying we need to pull back and get some perspective. Life is more important than our car breaking down. More important than kids not getting into the school of their choice. More important than what happens to our 401(k).

Jesus continues in the book of Matthew: "Look at the birds of the air; they do not sow or reap or store away in barns, and yet your heavenly Father feeds them. Are you not much more valuable than they?" (6:26 NIV).

Have you ever watched a bird? My friends regularly make fun of my bird-watching hobby. I don't know why I like watching them, but there is something peaceful about watching them spread their wings and take flight. I know, I know, I'm like an eighty-year-old man trapped in a younger body. But I love it.

If you watch birds for long, you discover that they really don't do a lot. They just seem to fly from tree to tree kind of aimlessly going through their day.

Ever had someone call you a birdbrain? It's not an endearing term, as birds are not the brightest animals in the kingdom. As a matter of fact, the majority of their little skull is actually made up of their eyeballs, leaving very little space for their brain.

But despite their seemingly lack of purpose and intellect, God takes care of them. Jesus is saying, "Hey, look at those birds. Don't you think that if God takes care of them and he knows about their plight that he knows about yours? Are you not much more valuable than a bird?

Then he drops this bomb: "Who of you by worrying can add a single hour to his life?" (6:27 NIV).

Jesus had this way of asking questions, which would just stop people dead in their tracks and force them to think about the core of their life.

Think about that question. Can anyone honestly say the time they've spent fearing the future or worrying about the unknown has added any length or value to their life?

Several years ago I was hiking with some buddies in Kentucky. We were out in the middle of the woods in the midst of this massive old farm. We had been told that there were several old farmhouses scattered throughout the property and were excited to find them and explore a bit.

Midway through the day we found one that sat in the middle of a huge valley. I'm sure at one time it had been all farmland surrounding this old home, but now it was just woods and thickets that had grown around it.

From the outside the old farmhouse actually looked like it was in pretty good condition. I was the first one of our group to crack open the old door and walk in. I couldn't wait to see the inside. I gingerly took three steps across the floor—and fell right through what used to be the living room floor. The home didn't look in that bad of shape, but beneath the surface, termites had been nibbling away.

Fear is not true to the way I've been wired. Faith is.

I think that describes a lot of us. We get up every day and walk into the world appearing for the most part to have it together. We parent, work, socialize, and continue to look as though we have it together, but beneath the surface termites of fear nibble away.

The Greek word *merimnao* translated to *worry* that is used throughout this passage literally means "to be drawn in different directions." This is what happens inside our minds when we worry and fear. It pulls us apart. It's a battle between the known and unknown.

I am inwardly fashioned for faith, not for fear and worry. Fear is not true to the way I've been wired. Faith is.

Now some may say this isn't true for you and that very time you face the unknown, you immediately revert to fear. That might be true, but it doesn't mean you were wired this way. It's the pattern your mind has developed over time. Your past has helped shape that habit.

Ever wonder why you feel so exhausted after a period of worry?

Ever wonder why fear just seems to drain you?

To live in this constant state of fear and worry is to live against the reality of our creation.

TRUST

Your fear comes from not trusting that God can take care of you. He identifies the problem with your fear of the unknown—it's a lack of faith as Jesus tells us in the book of Matthew: "And why do you worry about clothes? See how the lilies of the field grow. They do not labor or spin. Yet I tell you that not even Solomon in all his splendor was dressed like one of these. If that is how God clothes the grass of the field, which is here today and tomorrow is thrown into the fire, will he not much more clothe you, O you of little faith?" (6:28–30 NIV). So the issue of fear is actually an issue of faith.

This takes us right back to the issue we've been talking about the past few chapters. We have to decide—am I going to follow the path of trying to "please" God or the path of "trusting" God?

I think fear is unavoidable. Fear in and of itself is not a problem; it's the lack of faith in the midst of fear that's a problem. And Jesus is saying the reason some are paralyzed by fear when we think about these things is not really because we have a fear problem. Instead, we have a faith problem when we don't trust our heavenly Father.

While I have certainly trusted my heavenly Father with my eternity, I often have a tough time trusting him with my tomorrow. What a horrible indictment on my faith! And I bet I'm not alone.

Just like everyone else, as Christians, we're fearing and worrying about things like real estate, health, money, our kids, our marriage. We all have the same worries and concerns and fears. As we bump into people who have the same worries, our response should be so different they are amazed. Not that we're not concerned but that we react differently to the uncertainty of the unknown because our hope is anchored elsewhere.

Going back to the gospel of Matthew, after Jesus identifies

the problem, he provides a solution: "But seek first his kingdom and his righteousness, and all these things will be given to you as well" (6:33 NIV). He's essentially saying he wants to invite us into an entirely different way of thinking and living. He wants us to seek *first* his kingdom and his righteousness. In other words, he wants us to seek his agenda for the world. This is a decision that God's will be done before our will. That his kingdom comes before ours. If we want to begin retraining our mind, we have to live out this verse.

PERFECT LOVE

There are plenty of things in this world that we should legitimately be concerned about—terrorists, natural disasters, car accidents, to name a few. But the beauty of following Christ is that concern doesn't have to become fear. Fear is born when we choose to believe life is out of control. We start to think God doesn't love us or care, or know what's going on in our life. That he won't come through for us.

> Fear is born when we choose to believe life is out of control.

The remedy to fear, as the apostle John tells us in 1 John 4:18, is perfect love. If we're afraid of facing a person or a situation in our life, God's love can help put our fears to rest.

Several years ago I met with a woman named Lezlie from our church. As we were sitting down, the first words out of her mouth were, "I really don't want to be here." I remember sarcastically thinking, *Well, what in the world makes you think I want to be here? I could think of about a dozen other things I'd rather be doing.*

It turned out that coming to chat with me was not her idea; it was her husband's. "Bert told me I needed to come talk to you or he wants a divorce." I suddenly realized that I actually was exactly where I needed to be.

Lezlie had been abused as a child and was fearful of being hurt or taken advantage of and extremely insecure. While there are many people, maybe some of you, walking around with the same wound, these wounds tend to get expressed in lots of different ways.

Lezlie had spent most of her adult life trying to control everything and everyone's life. She was exhausted trying to control her two teenage daughters and had, over time, pushed her husband Bert far away. He had expressed that he couldn't take it anymore. She corrected every little thing he said. She interrupted his conversations. She'd hit the roof if he was five minutes late home from work.

As Lezlie and I talked and prayed that day, it became clear that instead of living a fear-dominated life that led her to controlling and manipulating people, she needed to learn to trust God.

That day I gave her a little phrase I say to myself: "There is a God and it's not me."

I had her say it ten times out loud that day, hoping it would stay with her. Lezlie needed to believe that God would do what he said he would do. But most of all, she needed to abide in his love.

God's love drives out fear.

You may be in a situation that you've never been in before, facing all kinds of new responsibilities. You may have needs that are beyond your resources and you are filled with fear, which is telling you that you aren't going to make it. You may feel that nobody else cares. But God cares.

God's love drives out fear. It has to be more than just a biblical fact and something we let in daily. Let love in. Let hope in. And let go of fear. There's no longer room for it.

I'm embarrassed to admit it, but even after a couple of decades of walking with God, I still find that when fear is dominating my life, it's almost always fed by me doubting God's love. You'd think that after seeing God work in my life over and over and over, I'd be convinced of his unfailing love.

It's just so easy to start to think, *If God really loved me, I would be in this or that situation. If he really loved me, he'd have rescued me from this potentially devastating situation by now.*

A verse I've gone back to time and time again in those moments of fear and doubt is, "For I am persuaded beyond doubt (am sure) that neither death nor life, nor angels nor principalities, nor things impending and threatening nor things to come, nor powers, nor height nor depth, nor anything else in all creation will be able to separate us from the love of God which is in Christ Jesus our Lord" (Rom. 8:38–39 AMP).

Fear is knocking on the door of your heart.

Doubt is whispering in your ear.

Insecurities are begging for full reign.

Reject them. Focus on the love of God, which drives out all fear, and let hope in.

13

LOVING DEEPLY

Just a little over a year ago my grandpa Wilson passed away. I feel extremely blessed that I had the opportunity to know my grandpa well into adulthood. He was a remarkable man, holding the same job for over sixty years.

At his funeral they had several large boards with pictures of his life. Some of the pictures showed my grandpa receiving awards, but most of them were just casual pictures showing him with my family.

I couldn't help but think about the hundreds of people who showed up to talk about how he had impacted their lives. Everyone from former employees, church friends, and even several waitresses from a restaurant he frequented.

I wish every one of you could experience the honor and privilege I had of being loved, believed in, and mentored by such an amazing man. My life will forever be changed because of his influence. My entire life was shaped by his love.

Our lives are often shaped by two groups of people:

1. Those who love us.
2. Those who hurt us.

God has given every human being an immense power. How we use that power, in many ways, will determine our destiny. We can either shape the people around us by intentionally or unintentionally hurting them, or we can shape their life through loving them. It's impossible to live having a neutral relational impact on the people around us. Love is weaved into the tapestry of every great story, including yours, including mine.

Love is weaved into the tapestry of every great story, including yours, including mine.

Unfortunately, this is a sensitive topic for many of us. As the phrase goes, "Hurt people, hurt people." Since most of us have a past marked with lots of hurt, we've in turn hurt other people. We know this and are aware of this. So we judge, convict, and sentence ourselves.

But it's never too late.

Sure we've hurt a lot of people in our past, but we have to release ourselves from yesterday's scenario. It's never too late to be what you might have been. It's never too late to love as we should've been loving all along.

So even though we all may have a reason to be judgmental, hateful, and hurtful, none of us has a reason to stay that way.

A CLEAR COMMAND

Life is one giant lesson in love. It's not about how much we get (acquisition), how much we do (accomplishment), or how much we earn (achievement). It's not about all the other things we're told life's about. God put us on earth to learn to love. We were created to receive love and give love.

Jesus says the two most important things in life are 1) learn to love God with all your heart, and 2) learn to love everybody else (Matt. 22:36–40). He says if you get that, you've got life. If you don't get that, you just wasted your life.

While the day you were born was understandably important, the day you discovered why you were born is arguably a close second. Never let your past keep you from pursuing what you know in your heart you were meant to do. And no matter what that is, I guarantee you at the center of it is love. Over and over again our culture will try to convince you that ruthless competition is the key to success, but Jesus reminds us that ruthless love is the purpose of our journey.

Love is what life's about. No qualifier. No almost.

Love is the name of the game. Love God. Love others.

This isn't the soft and wimpy approach, diminishing the gospel; this is the whole game. As God loves us so are we to love others. This theme dominates the entire New Testament. For example, Jesus said, "You have heard that it was said, 'Love your neighbor and hate your enemy.' But I tell you, love your enemies and pray for those who persecute you, that you may be children of your Father in heaven" (Matt. 5:43–45 NIV). The apostle Peter tells us, "Most important of all, continue to show deep love for each other, for love covers a multitude of sins" (1 Peter 4:8). If we really took the Bible seriously, believed what it says about love, and acted on it, Christianity would have a much better reputation.

There's no doubt in my mind that I'm a Christian today because a couple of key Christians I was lucky enough to have in my life thought these verses were to be taken seriously. None of them always followed through or did so perfectly when they did, and everyone failed at one time or another. But as far as I know, each and every one of them thought this was the ideal toward which we should aim. They believed that without love for one another, all our theological precision, our faith, our speaking, and even our giving, is for nothing.

> Focusing on sinning less doesn't guarantee you will love more, but focusing on loving more will always guarantee that you will sin less.

In the book of John, Jesus defines discipleship for us and gives us a model to go on: "A new command I give you: Love one another. As I have loved you, so you must love one another. By this everyone will know that you are my disciples, if you love one another" (John 13:34–35 NIV).

This new command leads to a life-changing question. If we truly want to begin seeking full healing over our past, we need to ask ourselves, *What does love require of me?*

What does love require of me in my conversations? In my broken relationship? At work? At home? On my campus?

It has been about two thousand years since Jesus walked this earth. We can look back at the history of Christianity, and for all the good, our past is still stained with horrors.

We can look back never doubting for a minute that if we had prioritized love over theological correctness, love over denominations, love over our own personal preferences, and just followed in the humble footsteps of the man so many of us have claimed to have given our lives to, this world we live in and the very lives we're living would be vastly different.

Focusing on sinning less doesn't guarantee you will love more, but focusing on loving more will always guarantee that you will sin less.

POWER OF WORDS

Many of your scars were created by a potent weapon that we all carry around with us.

A good friend of mine recently purchased a handgun. He doesn't plan on actually carrying it, but he still took the concealed weapon class. It's a required class for those who want to obtain a permit to carry a concealed weapon. This is a good idea, because an individual with a gun who doesn't know how to use it could cause a lot of damage without even meaning to.

There's a force that can be equally as damaging as a gun because it means life or death not just to the body but to the soul, and every human being is issued one at birth.

It's called the mouth.

Proverbs says, "The tongue has the power of life and death, and those who love it will eat its fruit" (Prov. 18:21 NIV).

Words are powerful. So much of our baggage—self-esteem, pride, trust, and envy—has been planted in our souls by the words that important people in our life used.

With words self-esteems are shaped. Wars started. Murders initiated. Divorces sealed. Children crushed. And while we are sensitive about the words that come to us, we are often careless about what comes out.

Scripture confirms the power of words. James 3 can be summed up like, *Warning! You have unbelievable potential to impact the people around you with your words.* "We all stumble in many ways. If anyone is never at fault in what he says, he is a perfect man, able to keep his whole body in check. When we put bits into the mouths of horses to make them obey us, we can turn the whole animal" (James 3:2–3 NIV).

In other words, if you put something that weighs a pound into its mouth, you can control a thousand-pound animal. You can change the direction of the horse if you have control of his mouth. The next example James gives is how a large ship is steered by a small rudder. Again, he's saying it's a small part but a big influence.

Then, consider how a great forest can be set on fire by a small spark. "The tongue also is a fire, a world of evil among the parts of the body. It corrupts the whole person, sets the whole course of his life on fire, and is itself set on fire by hell. All kinds of animals, birds, reptiles, and creatures of the sea are being tamed and have been tamed by man, but no man can tame the tongue. It is a restless evil, full of deadly poison" (vv. 6–8 NIV).

We just added a rescue dog to our family. He's one and a half and as far as veterinarians can tell, he has never lived with a human family. He's as wild as they come, so we've been in the process of training him. Over the past couple of weeks he's actually learned to use the bathroom outside. You can tame your dog to pee outside and pretty much you don't have to ever worry about them again. Not so with your mouth. You can't tame it and then never worry about it again. It's something we have to be consciously aware of.

A GAUGE OF HEALTH

Now Jesus had some pretty interesting things to say about our words as well: "You brood of vipers, how can you who are evil say anything good? For out of the overflow of the heart the mouth speaks" (Matt. 12:34 NIV). The real issue is, if we have a mouth problem, we have a heart problem.

Have you ever said something and then followed it up with, "I don't know where that came from"? I do. Your heart. That is the real issue.

Because whatever is going on in my heart, over time is eventually going to come out of my mouth. And I can try to work by willpower real hard on my mouth, but if my heart doesn't change, inevitably, my mouth is going to lead. This is huge for those of us who are trying to get a gauge on just how free we are from our past.

Now it's easy to start to think that if our mouth gets us in that much trouble, maybe we should just quit talking altogether. But I believe God's goal is something much bigger than you just not saying mean things.

God's goal for the human race is not just that we avoid sin. That was the problem with the Pharisees. That was the problem with legalism. God's goal for his creation is not just avoidance—there could be no sin going on at all in creation and that would not bring delight to God. God's goal in your healing is for there to be an explosion of goodness and joy and love.

> The real issue is, if we have a mouth problem, we have a heart problem.

And if you never talked, there would never be any expression of life, creative ideas, or articulation of hope.

So, God's goal for you is way more than just avoiding verbal sin. As devastating as your words can be to a human soul, I believe they can be equally as life-giving if used in the right way. People's words can be the fuel that carries you through your life.

There is an element of power in our words, and it's not accidental. He shaped our hearts and souls to be impacted by the words of others. And because our words will have a shelf life with all who hear them, they also have the ability to shape life.

This is not accidental; it's part of your design.

God has designed the human soul in such a way that your words will either destroy or build up one another. We read in Ephesians to "not let any unwholesome talk come out of your mouths, but only what is helpful for building others up according to their needs, that it may benefit those who listen" (4:29 NIV).

Use your words in a way that they are helpful for building others up—"according to their needs." This implies an element of awareness. We need to know what their needs are, and we need to have a level of attentiveness.

I will tell you a little secret about all the people that God allows you to lock eyes with. Whether it's your neighbor, your spouse, your coworker, or the person sitting next to you right now.

> God has designed the human soul in such a way that your words will either destroy or build up one another.

No matter how well put together everyone looks, everybody needs healing. Your words can bring healing to them.

The natural question: Who has God placed in your life? And what do they need to hear you say?

Husbands, what does your wife need to hear you say? Maybe it's as simple as you saying, "Honey, I just want you to know that you're an incredible gift from God." You might think to yourself, *Well, she knows I love her.* But she still needs to hear it. There is power in words.

Wives, what does your husband need to hear you say?

What do your children need to hear you say?

What do the people you lead and manage at work need to hear? What do they need to hear you say? When is the last time you looked them in the eye and told them how much they mean to you? You may think to yourself, *Well, that's why we pay them.* No, you're missing the point. There is power in words.

I know sometimes we are not comfortable with this. Some of you grew up in a family where feelings like this weren't shared.

Some of you would say I'm just not used to that level of communication. I understand. But your choice of comfort over using your words to build people up is a tragic choice.

Who is one person in your life that desperately needs to hear something from you? I know you have baggage. I know your dad didn't do this. I know your family didn't share in this way. I know this might be weird for you. But if you want to receive healing and give healing, you'll do it.

God has created an element of power in my words and has designed others' souls in such a way that they need to hear those words. And when you use your words to build people up, they will flow from your mouth and land on their soul.

PRACTICAL

Besides using my words strategically, I've discovered there are a few other practical choices I can make every day. In fact, I've discovered that if I make a decision to do these three things each day before my feet even hit the floor, it sets me up well to extend love in a healing way.

1. FIND VALUE IN EVERY PERSON

I'm a pastor so I'm around a lot of other pastors. I speak at a lot of church conferences, so sometimes I get to have conversations with dozens and dozens of pastors in one day. And I've noticed something about us pastors. We (like a lot of other people) find our own personal value by devaluing the other pastors around us.

Isn't it funny how we can agree with 90 percent of what someone says, but we focus on, tweet about, and write blog posts concerning the other 10 percent?

And just so I'm clear by "funny," I really mean sad and pathetic. Why do we do this?

Why do we poke fun?

Why do we criticize?

We usually do it because we somehow think it justifies our stance. Because surely we couldn't both be right. Surely more than one model wouldn't work.

We usually do it because our ego has been damaged, and it just makes us feel better to tear someone else down. I hate this part of me, but I know from experience tearing others down can briefly make me feel better about myself.

We usually do it because we ourselves have been a victim of criticism, and we're reacting from our hurt. Remember, hurt people, hurt people. We're just doing what we know.

Jesus addresses this in the book of Matthew: "And why worry about a speck in your friend's eye when you have a log in your own? How can you think of saying to your friend, 'Let me help you get rid of that speck in your eye,' when you can't see past the log in your own eye? Hypocrite! First get rid of the log in your own eye; then you will see well enough to deal with the speck in your friend's eye" (7:3–5).

Instead of focusing on the 10 percent we don't agree with, why don't we build relationships based on the 90 percent of what we do?

Can I make a suggestion? Instead of focusing on the 10 percent we don't agree with, why don't we build relationships based on the 90 percent of what we do? We need to show love to others, and offer grace when needed.

Trust me. I don't agree with everything my pastor friends believe. I don't believe in all of their theology, strategies, personalities, and models, but I've found we're still on the same team and can accomplish a lot more together than we can tearing each other apart.

The same goes for you, and the people you're around. If listening to that person's podcast ticks you off, then don't listen. If every time you read someone's facebook update, you find yourself fighting a wave of jealousy, then stop reading it.

I know some may be wondering about how to bring about change if we don't challenge, question, and push back. But there's a way to do so that contains respect, love, and grace. There is a way we can engage in a conversation without throwing stones and taking public shots at each other.

Focus on the change you need to bring to your life, to your sphere of influence. Worry about the "log" and give the "speck" a break.

Our firestorms of criticism are doing immense damage to the body of Christ. Not only are we distracting each other from our main mission, we are simply playing right into the hands of those outside the faith who already think we're trite and hypocritical.

To love in a way that it heals so many of the negative, critical patterns of our past, we have to believe that every person in the world has intrinsic value and then look for it. Understand that their perspective is unique to them, and that is beneficial. Seek what is helpful instead of being focused on what we find offensive. Always be asking, "What can they teach me?" I learn so much from people who think differently than I do.

2. OVERCOME SELF-CENTEREDNESS

Having hurt feelings and being easily offended is almost always a result of being too preoccupied with "self":

No one liked *my* ideas.

He hardly talked to *me*.

They didn't even thank *me*.

Why wasn't *I* considered for the position?

The it's-all-about-me mentality is fertile soil for being frequently offended. If every word out of every mouth, every action or inaction, all that is done or undone, all motives and intentions become a reflection of you, it's a huge burden to carry.

The it's-all-about-me mentality is fertile soil for being frequently offended.

If everything is reduced to how it affects you, if you reside at the center of everything, no wonder you are offended so frequently!

Move away from the center of everyone else's life. Your friend's bad mood isn't about you; it's about them. Your mom's guilt trip isn't even about you either; it's about her!

As the apostle Paul wrote, "Do nothing out of selfish ambition or vain conceit. Rather, in humility value others above yourselves" (Phil. 2:3 NIV). Once we stop being so preoccupied with ourselves, we won't be so easily offended and can instead focus on loving others.

3. LOVE PEOPLE MORE THAN BEING RIGHT

If you value people more than you do your pride (which is fed with the idea of being right), then opposition to your thoughts and beliefs will be inoffensive no matter how offensive the other person is trying to be.

Reasons to find offense surround us. We need to look no further than our bosses, employees, misguided pastors, high-maintenance family members, political candidates, and the list goes on.

When we see things we do not like, we feel we have no choice but to become upset—and express it adamantly. We view our response as outside of our hands. We are only reacting to others.

Like most things, however, offense is really an issue of the self. It has nothing to do with the person who is offending you and everything to do with you, your past, and your wounds. When you choose to not be offended, you have taken the first step toward external influence and internal healing.

DON'T BE CONFUSED

Sometimes people think they are growing spiritually or healing from their past simply because they attend more church services or know more about the Bible. But their hearts, especially for people who are far from God, grow a little bit colder year after year.

Jesus clarified this confusion for us in a conversation he had one day with the Pharisees: "But the Pharisees and the teachers of the law who belonged to their sect complained to his disciples, 'Why do you eat and drink with tax collectors and sinners?' Jesus answered them, 'It is not the healthy who need a doctor, but the sick. I have not come to call the righteous, but sinners to repentance'" (Luke 5:30–32 NIV).

Searching after people far from God is not something Jesus did in addition to being spiritually mature and whole. It is what Jesus did *precisely* because he was spiritually mature and whole. Jesus' plan for winning the whole world is to make each person he touches magnetic enough with love to draw others in. Now it's our turn.

Those of us who have been rescued, healed, and restored by the grace of Jesus understand that we then turn our hearts and lives toward rescuing and restoring those who need it. It's time for the rescued to rescue the thousands who need healing and restoration.

We need to pursue those who are addicted, those who are lost, those who are hurting, those who need a second chance.

You're up.

A REVERSE ECONOMY

Things that go wrong can shape us or scar us. Like many of you, I've had some people love me well in my life and some people who did not love so well.

I've probably had more love me than not, but I'm working hard not to keep score anymore. In fact, I've found a tremendous amount of healing power in loving people regardless of how much or how little they've loved me. It makes all the difference between my interaction with them shaping me or scarring me. Love is meant to heal.

It can heal the anger you have toward your father.

It can heal the guilt you have for not giving your children love when they needed it.

It can heal the hurt you have over losing a friend.

Love aids recovery. Nobody would argue that receiving love brings healing in every aspect of your life. I believe, however, that extending love may in fact hold more healing power than receiving it.

In the Gospels, Jesus was always talking about a reverse economy.

If you want to receive, you give.

If you want to lead, you follow.

If you want to live for certain things, you have to be willing to die for them.

Don't ask me to explain this, because I can't tell you how or why. All I can say is that I know because I have experienced it. I've been there, and that is all the proof I can provide. It won't be enough for some of you. It won't be the kind of thing you can accept because you can't buy, touch, or taste it.

But there's unexplainable healing, peace, and life found in extending the love that God has lavished freely upon us. Extend it to anyone and everyone regardless of whether they deserve it or not.

Jesus did not just come to save us from our sin, but to save us for the kind of life we were created to live. To save us for lives that make a radical difference in our world. Every life was created to make a difference.

Jesus helps us do this through love.

14

TRUSTING FULLY

Years ago I met Mac at the gym. Mac and I were about the same age, both married, and both had small children at home. For months we would bump into each other at the gym a couple of times a week and just chat about the weather, kids, and politics in between lifting sets of weights. I never told him what I did, and for some reason it just never came up.

One Tuesday Mac wasn't there, which was strange because I always saw him there regardless of what day I showed up. I asked a couple of the other guys if they had seen him earlier, and one of them said they heard Mac's wife had been taken to the hospital over the weekend. I did a little digging and someone at the gym gave me Mac's cell phone number, so I gave him a call.

Luckily, his wife's medical issue was not life threatening, but Mac told me she would be there a few more days. I took this opportunity to tell him that I was a pastor and that I'd like to come up and visit them if they didn't mind.

The next night I went up there and spent some time with him and his wife and prayed for her. Her parents were at the hospital visiting, so I asked Mac if he wanted to go down to the cafeteria to grab some dinner. I think he was pretty tired of being cooped up in the hospital room, so he was more than happy to join me.

We sat down over some mediocre hospital food, and the very first thing he said was, "So you're a pastor, huh?"

I said, "Yep, I am." An awkwardly long silence followed.

Eventually Mac cut to the chase. "Pete, I don't want to offend you, but I'm not sure I really believe anymore. It's hard for me to imagine that there's not some kind of God who created this whole world, but I don't believe he's really involved in our lives."

"What makes you think that?" I asked.

Mac went on to tell me that Karen was actually his second wife. He got married the first time when he was just twenty-one. His first wife was very involved in church, and so the two of them served together and were quite active.

One day after three years of marriage, out of the blue, she came home and told him she wanted a divorce. She had fallen in love and was having an affair with a mutual friend of theirs from church.

Mac said, "Over the next six to eight weeks I lost over fifty pounds. I was so distraught I couldn't eat or work. I ended up losing my job, most of my friends, and my faith. During that season I prayed and prayed for God to bring her back to me. I remember saying out loud, 'God, if you exist, please just do this one thing. Heal my marriage. Allow her to love me like she used to love me.' It never happened and I've not been back to church since."

"Mac, do you ever pray?" I asked.

"Sometimes."

"Who do you pray to when you pray?"

He replied, "That's just it. I don't know. I don't even know why I pray, because I don't really believe he hears or cares anymore."

Mac reminds me of a lot of different people I've met over the years. They believe in the idea of a God; they just don't think he's intimately involved in their life. And often they've drawn that conclusion because their idea of God doesn't line up with something that's happened in their past.

The trust that drives us to new beginnings and sustained life change is less a matter of faith in the existence of God than it is a practical trust in his loving care regardless of what's happened in our past. Will I trust God's grace? His healing? His presence? Will I trust him to use it all for my best and his glory?

DEALING WITH DOUBTS

Throughout this book we have been asking some difficult questions:

What do you do when your past isn't really your past?

What do you do when life doesn't turn out the way you thought it would?

What do you do when God doesn't show up for you like you thought he would?

What do you do when someone hurts you intentionally and you can't seem to forgive that person?

While I can't give you a specific answer to those questions, I do know that we all are going to get to that place where life hurts and our hearts are broken. We

> We all are going to get to that place where life hurts and our hearts are broken.

are going to find ourselves in the middle of what I call a "Plan B."

Christianity cannot always be reduced to a simple answer. Some of you thought when you became a Christian that you would gain all the answers to life's difficulties. Here is a reality check and hopefully a pressure release for some of you: Just because we are Christians doesn't mean we know how to respond to everything that comes our way. We don't have all the answers.

In Brennan Manning's book *Ruthless Trust,* he tells the story of the brilliant ethicist John Kavanaugh who went to work for three months at "the house of the dying" in Calcutta. He was seeking a clear answer as to how best to spend the rest of his life. On the first morning there he met Mother Teresa who asked, "And what can I do for you?" Kavanaugh asked her to pray for him. "What do you want me to pray for?" she asked. He voiced the request that he had borne thousands of miles from the United States: "Pray that I have clarity." She said firmly, "No, I will not do that." When he asked her why, she said, "Clarity is the last thing you are clinging to and must let go of." When Kavanaugh commented that she always seemed to have the clarity he longed for, she laughed and said, "I have never had clarity; what I have always had is trust. So I will pray that you trust God."[1]

The reality is, we often have more questions than we do answers. Sometimes we lack the faith that will give us sustained hope. Even though we know God is with us, sometimes we feel utterly and completely alone.

The reality is, even though we know, we doubt.

TWO TYPES OF HOPE

There are two very different types of hope in this world. One is hoping *for something*, and the other is hoping *in someone*.

Eventually everything we hope for will disappoint us. Every circumstance, every situation that we're hoping for is going to wear out, fall apart, melt down, and go away. When that happens, the question then is about your deeper hope, your foundational hope, your fallback hope when all your other hopes have disappointed.

All of Scripture points to one man, one God, not because he gives us everything we're hoping for but because he is the One we put our hope in.

I know this book will fall short of helping you find life-changing transformation if all we do is identify the problems, challenges, and painful moments of your past. Identifying these memories from your past alone doesn't help you. If all you do is remember the source of your pain, then something has gone horribly wrong. Why drudge up the past if you can't find healing from the pain?

And for there to be real healing, for your past to really become your past, what needs to happen here is that you discover or discern the lie that your memory contains. This is fundamental to your healing.

It is important to understand that your past is not really the problem. The real problem is the lie you believed when an event happened in your past.

The truth is that memories don't hurt us. It is what we believe about those memories that hurts us. For Mac, it wasn't the memory of his ex-wife leaving him that was keeping him from truly beginning again. It was the belief that God abandoned him when his ex-wife left him. Choosing to believe that false lie about his past was devastating for him.

The truth is that memories don't hurt us. It is what we believe about those memories that hurts us.

Trusting in the loving care of God regardless of what has happened in my past has been an ongoing process in my journey. And it's only when we trust his loving care that we're able to really begin to allow the hope of Christ to shine through us.

Yes, hurt people do hurt people. But what's equally true is that free people free people. And becoming free starts with being able to fully trust the loving care of God despite what we've possibly been through in our past.

Recently there's been a series of prayers that I've been praying, which have tremendously helped me to fully trust in God.

PRAYER #1: GIVE ME A GREATER VIEW OF YOU

A couple of weeks ago I was reading John 15: "I am the true vine, and my Father is the gardener" (v. 1 NIV). I've spent a lot of time thinking and even preaching about the fact that Jesus is the "vine," but I had never thought about the fact that Jesus says that his Father, our God, is the "gardener."

I'm a self-proclaimed garden expert and have had a garden every year since I was twenty-three. Every year I plant corn, green beans, squash, cucumbers, pumpkins, onions, potatoes, and just about any other vegetable you can think of. Right now it's winter, so I don't have anything planted. But I'm still gardening. I'm going through seed catalogs, trying to select what will be best to plant in a few months. I'm composting so that I can make my soil rich enough to support what I want to grow.

> The single most important thing in our minds is our idea of God.

Here's what I know: A good gardener will do whatever it takes to make the garden thrive.

As the gardener, God wants me to thrive. He wants me to live with hope. He wants me to move beyond my past. So I'm praying, "God, give me a greater view of you. Help me see you for who you really are." When we see God as the gardener, whether we're in adversity or joy, tribulation or relief, we can put an unfaltering trust in his love, his care, and his plan.

The single most important thing in our minds is our idea of God. When we discover that God is good, we find ourselves being able to trust him and taking risks for him we wouldn't take before.

I was in college when I first sensed God prompting me to go into ministry. I was scared that I would be miserable as a pastor because I didn't see myself fitting in with the church. I was scared to tell Brandi. We were engaged and she didn't sign up to marry a pastor. I was scared because it wasn't at all what I had planned. I was scared because I had a past and not all parts of that past were pretty. Could God still use me in spite of all that?

But throughout my college years I became more and more aware of God's goodness, and while I didn't know how it was all going to turn out, I knew I could trust in him. Throughout my life God has called me to trust him in some things that made absolutely no sense to me, but I could trust him because I know that God is good.

When God said launch a church in the middle of nowhere Kentucky, I could trust him because he is good.

When Brandi and I didn't have two nickels to rub together, we could continue to tithe and be generous as God's Word called us to be because he is good.

When God called me to leave that church that I was in love with and move back to Nashville, I could trust him because he is good.

When Brandi had a miscarriage and we were mad and upset and felt alone, I could still trust him and turn to him because he is good. I don't always understand, but he is good.

GOING DEEPER

The complaint I've heard the most from people at church is that they want to go deeper. While this means different things to different people, I've always thought this complaint was a bit silly—it's basically Christians who don't think their pastor's teaching is "deep" enough.

While there are a lot of really good excuses to leave a church, I think in most cases this isn't one of them. The overwhelming majority of us are educated—we know the Greek words and historical background. In fact, we've got enough insight to last a lifetime. What we need is to trust what we've already received. Most of us are educated far beyond our obedience.

Whether you're new to the spiritual journey or you've been a follower of Jesus for decades, the response he seeks is always the same: trust.

And you can trust God—he's good and trustworthy. He's the gardener and wants you to thrive.

PRAYER #2: IS THERE ANYTHING IN MY LIFE THAT NEEDS TO BE PRUNED?

Immediately after Jesus' declaration in John 15 that God is the gardener he says, "He cuts off every branch in me that bears no fruit, while every branch that does bear fruit he prunes so that it will be even more fruitful" (v. 2 NIV).

Asking God to prune or cut out things in your life is not the easiest of prayers. This isn't the kind of prayer you're going to see on a T-shirt or church slogan. It's tough. But remember he's the gardener. If he's pruning, it's for your good. It's so you can thrive and grow.

In order to fully trust God, you must be willing to invite and welcome the pruning process. You must be willing to go before him with a desire to give him anything and everything.

Several years ago I went through a season where I felt compelled to pray "the pruning prayer" every day for several weeks. Not sure why, it was just one of those prompts and I'm so glad I did. After several weeks of praying "God, is there anything in my life you want or need to prune?" I got a very clear prompt from God.

What I sensed God saying was, *Pete, I want you to give up your need for the approval of other people.*

Few things will wear you down like trying to control your image in the eyes of other people. I don't know about you, but I have definitely found myself in this trap, caring too much about what people think of me. I was spending so much energy project-ing and predicting and wondering what impression I'm making that I had lost track of the really important question: Am I doing what God has called and designed me to do?

> In order to fully trust God, you must be willing to invite and welcome the pruning process.

In this season I had found myself in an uncomfortable position at the church I pastor in Nashville. The church was growing fast, and my responsibilities as pastor were shifting. I could no longer personally minister to all the people who called Cross Point home. But I stubbornly kept trying to do all the counseling, all the weddings, all the mes-sages, and all the meetings. This schedule left me so depleted that I had very little time or energy left for my family and friends.

At the time, I thought my attempts to be all things to all people came from a desire to be loving. I now look back and realize the reason God wanted to prune was that my primary motivation was not to be loving but to be loved. And there is a huge difference between the two, isn't there?

I discovered that if I really wanted to be loving, I needed to allow the other pastors on our staff to step up and minister. That was a difficult transition for me because for years I had derived so much of my validation from the pats on the back I received from church members. But I've gradually learned to treasure what happens when I let myself step back and depend on God for my validation.

More people are served.

More people know the joy of using their gifts in ministry.

My important relationships—with my wife, my children, my close friends, and my God—have room to grow. I feel energized

> Because God is the gardener, I can invite him to prune knowing he has my best interest in mind.

instead of exhausted and depleted. And because I'm tapping into the Source of dependable love, I feel more valued and confident.

Because God is the gardener, I can invite him to prune knowing he has my best interest in mind. His cutting out, his chiseling, his pruning is not meant to damage as much as it's meant to help me flourish. So in this process I can trust him.

As a child growing up in church, one of my all-time favorite Bible stories was the account of the little boy with two fish and five loaves. Remember the following story?

A huge crowd kept following [Jesus] wherever he went, because they saw his miraculous signs as he healed the sick. Then Jesus climbed a hill and sat down with his disciples around him. (It was nearly time for the Jewish Passover celebration.) Jesus soon saw a huge crowd of people coming to look for him. Turning to Philip, he asked, "Where can we buy bread to feed all these people?" He was testing Philip, for he already knew what he was going to do. Philip replied, "Even if we worked for months, we wouldn't have enough money to feed them!" (John 6:2–7)

I love Philip's response. That's so me. I'm so quick to respond with the excuses for my inability to do whatever it is Jesus has asked of me.

Forgive them?

Love them?

Be generous to them?

Trust you?

Well, I would, but I just don't see that it's going to be possible. God, I'm not sure you understand what I'm really feeling or what I'm really going through.

Then Andrew, Simon Peter's brother, spoke up. "There's a young boy here with five barley loaves and two fish. But what good is that with this huge crowd?" (vv. 8–9).

Even here Andrew fired back with yet another reason to do nothing. But Jesus took the food and gave some to everyone so that they could eat what they wanted. "After everyone was full, Jesus told his disciples, 'Now gather the leftovers, so that nothing is wasted.' So they picked up the pieces and filled twelve baskets with scraps left by the people who had eaten from the five barley loaves" (vv. 12–13).

This kid brought what he had. No more, no less. Now let's be clear about this. Jesus didn't need the kid. He didn't need the two fish and five loaves. He could've turned two rocks and five branches into lunch for everyone, but he didn't. He used what the kid offered voluntarily.

He took the two fish and five loaves and used it to take care of the needs of the entire crowd. With Jesus 1 + 1 doesn't equal 2. Jesus says *just bring me what you have*. And he does the unthinkable. You'll never know what God can do with what you have until you bring it to him. That's why I love partnering my life with him.

Regardless of how my life turns out, I'll be glad I was a person of faith. I'll be glad I prayed and invited God, the gardener, to prune away. I'll be glad I trusted him with all that I have and all that I am.

The Bible reminds us that this life is a vapor. It's true, but I want to live my life in a way that it's a vapor worth celebrating. I'm going to believe big and trust big with no regrets. What's the alternative? Walking around living a small life of insignificance because I only attempted things I could pull off or understand on my own. No thanks. I want to give God what I have and watch him do what only he can do.

PRAYER #3: GIVE ME HEROIC COURAGE

One day when I was a kid I was playing with a group of kids in my neighborhood. We ended up over at my friend Rob's house who had a huge two-story deck coming off the back of his house. To this day I still don't know what in the world made us think this was a good idea, but someone suggested we jump off that deck.

I remember standing up there thinking it was deathly high. Nobody really wanted to jump off the towering deck, but we had somehow convinced each other this was the ultimate stunt of bravery. For what seemed like hours, we stood up there talking about jumping. Eventually I couldn't take it anymore so I jumped. I remember hitting the ground and just rolling down his backyard.

Despite the jolt I received when I landed, and a few scrapes from rolling, I was fine. All the kids in the neighborhood came barreling down the steps (which was the smart way to descend from the deck) to check on me. I still remember everyone giving me high fives. I would like to tell you that they carried me home on their shoulders that day, but I'm pretty sure I've added that part to my memory over the years. I do know for a moment I was on top of the world. It felt good to have heroic courage. Even as kids, we will go to great lengths so people think we are strong and courageous.

> He's talking about telling the truth because that takes courage.

A few months ago, along with millions of others, I watched an Austrian man named Felix Baumgartner set the world record for skydiving. When he leaped from his capsule, he was literally on the edge of space some 128,000 feet above the earth (twenty-four miles in the air).

Many of us tend to associate courage with extreme and extraordinary action, but when God says, "I want you to be strong and courageous," he's usually not talking about an extreme sports kind of courage; he's talking about everyday courage.

He's talking about telling the truth because that takes courage.

He's talking about a single parent trying to raise a child.

He's talking about someone who finally has the guts to ask for help.

He's talking about loving someone who everyone else has characterized as unlovable.

He's talking about a person who has never tithed before—never trusted God with their finances—finally trusting God in that area.

He's talking about stepping out in faith and trusting God in some area of your life that scares you to death.

●　●　●

One of my favorite movies is *We Bought a Zoo*. (I get made fun of all the time for my taste in movies. *The Bodyguard* is another favorite.) In *We Bought a Zoo* widowed dad Benjamin Mee, played by Matt Damon, is working to instill a sense of courage and adventure in his children. They are dealing with a great loss and a big transition in their lives, so Benjamin feels the responsibility of equipping his children to tackle life head on. He sums this philosophy up in one scene by saying to his son, "You know, sometimes all you need is twenty seconds of insane courage. Just literally twenty seconds of just embarrassing bravery. And I promise you, something great will come of it."

For most of us, it's risky to let go of our past and to move out from a comfortable place into the scary unknown. It takes courage to forgive, relinquish old hurts, and give up bitterness and resentment, especially if those have become our comfort patterns over the years. It takes courage to fully trust God—to trust him with your past, to trust that he's with you every step of the way, to receive his grace. But if you will, I promise you something great will come of it.

The decisions of everyday courage may not be glamorous or noticeable. No one is going to post them on YouTube; but they take courage nonetheless. These are the decisions that have a huge impact on who we're becoming. This kind of heroic courage is part of the art of new beginnings.

> We can't live without hope. When we keep hoping, we keep living.

To fully trust is a rare and precious thing. Few people ever get to this place of heroic courage. When your past is littered with failure, rejection, abandonment, betrayal, or loneliness, it requires heroic courage to trust in the love of God no matter what happens to us.

Some of you are still surrounded by the walls of your past. You can't see beyond it. And as a result you've lost all perspective. All you see are the hurdles and obstacles to living the life you had imagined. But if you can get the walls to come down, you will see a hope you never thought existed.

We can't live without hope. When we keep hoping, we keep living.

Most of us take a peek through the cracks in the walls to catch a glimpse of what's possible on the other side. What keeps us from tearing the walls down? Fear of what's on the other side?

The power to unleash you is in your daring trust of God. Dare to believe that he will do what he said he would do. Shift your confidence from your own weaknesses to his power. Trust in him rather than in yourself.

Believe that he will satisfy every need created by your history. You have nothing to lose and everything to gain. Jesus will heal the broken places of your heart and make you completely whole. When you allow him access to every area of your life, you will never be the same broken person again.

We're reminded in 2 Corinthians 5:17, "Therefore, if anyone is in Christ, he is a new creation; the old has gone, the new has come!"(NIV).

THE DEATH OF DEATH

The Bible gives us many of the difficult details concerning the death of Jesus. From his hands and feet being nailed to the cross, to the soldiers gambling over his clothes. We're told in the gospel of Matthew that "darkness fell across the whole land."

That was the first day, a dark day for many reasons. His followers were crushed. They had seen the glory for a while, and now it was gone. Hope was lying in a tomb.

The second day, Saturday, didn't look any better. On the second day, Pontius Pilate posted a guard to stand watch over the tomb, because he was in control now. He wanted to make sure nothing happened, that nobody came in and did anything funny.

We don't talk a lot about Saturday. We spend a lot of time talking about Good Friday, the day of redemption because the blood of Jesus was shed. We also spend time celebrating Easter Sunday, the day Jesus conquered death so we can have life. It doesn't get any better than Easter Sunday. But we don't hear a lot about Saturday, a day that nothing happened. It seems almost as if God forgot on that dark and disappointing day.

But the story of Jesus is a Three-Day Story.

The Third Day is God's day.

The Third Day is when rivers are parted and people enter the Promised Land.

The Third Day is when young girls like Esther face down powerful, giant kings.

The Third Day is when prophets like Jonah are dropped off at seaside ports by giant fish.

The Third Day is the day stones are rolled away.

The Third Day is when a crucified carpenter came back to life, defeating death and giving us a hope beyond all hopes.

The Third Day is a reminder that God does his best work in hopeless situations.

We worship a God who specializes in resurrections in the ultimate hopeless situation. He conquered death, so we could have life. Jesus' disciples saw him risen and everything changed. They went from hopeless to hopeful, powerless to powerful. There was this unstoppable force of hope in them that allowed them to go on to help change the world.

And some of you would say, "Well, good for them." No, good for us.

Good for me.

Good for you.

Good for anyone who is in desperate need of hope today. The resurrection is more than just a historical reality. We don't gather this weekend all around the world just to celebrate a moment in history. We gather together to say what happened two thousand years ago changed this world forever. It changed my life forever.

> My hope is based on a God who can do and will do the impossible.

I can have hope in the midst of my crisis. I can have hope when there is no circumstantial reason to have hope, because my hope is not based on what the stock market does, on what you think of me, on life turning out the way I want life to turn out.

My hope is based on a God who can do and will do the impossible. My hope is based on a God who has defeated death itself. The apostle Paul tells us that we will "understand the incredible greatness of God's power for us who believe him. This is the same mighty power that raised Christ from the dead and seated him in the place of honor at God's right hand in the heavenly realms" (Eph. 1:19–20).

The same power that was at work in Christ is now at work in those who believe him. Most people don't just go there. Most people want to believe in a lot of other things that might give them hope, but it can't be manufactured.

Your lust, your anger, your bitterness, that stuff that has been following you around for years—you don't possess the power to fix it. You don't have the power to raise to life that which was dead. You can't resurrect anything.

But Christ can. And the power of Christ is available to you and in you. You are not helpless and hopeless, and the resurrection doesn't just affect eternity.

It impacts right here, right now.

It impacts this world, this life.

Resurrection announces that God hasn't given up on us. He hasn't given up on you. He's making all things new. When your life has been destroyed and it feels as though you could never recover from your past, hope is on its way. Will you believe? Will you trust? Will you let it in?

EPILOGUE
Don't Miss Out

As we near the end of this book, I hope that you have come to see yourself in the same light as Joseph, who we started with. No matter what's been said to you, no matter what's been done to you, nothing can be taken away from who God has made you to be.

You may be in a very scary place right now, but that can change. Your brothers may have beat you up, threw you into a pit, sold you into slavery, and pretended you were dead. God is a God of transformation and resurrection. He has a future for you that you have never dreamed of because you thought you didn't deserve it. You may find yourself second in command over all of Egypt.

The truth is, you don't deserve God's goodness. None of us do. God's goodness is a gift. When you learn to view your painful life events through the filter of truth instead of the filter of lies, you'll find that you are producing an entirely different kind of fruit. Instead of denial and shame, you will produce what the Bible calls peace and joy. And instead of being known by shame, you will be known by grace.

When you begin to realize that your past does not necessarily dictate the outcome of your future, you can release the hurt. It is impossible to inhale new air until you exhale the old. I pray that as you continue on your journey, as you continue to work through the four choices I've presented in this book, God will give you the grace of releasing you from where you have been so you can receive what God has for you now.

Inside all of us is a pull toward regret.

Inside all of us is a tug toward fear.

Inside all of us is a desire for hope.

Deep within you, nothing is hopeless. You are a child of God, and he has planted hope in you. Let go of the regret and fear, and instead focus on the hope. Focus on the desire, and let hope in.

ACKNOWLEDGMENTS

To my parents—Thank you for your constant support and love. Your belief in me has given me the confidence to chase after my dreams.

To Jett, Gage, and Brewer—You boys have no idea how much you're teaching me these days. I'm having the time of my life watching you three grow up. Never forget that I love you with all my heart.

To my Cross Point Church family—Thank you for allowing me to serve you. You guys blow me away with the radical love and grace you consistently show people in the Nashville area. You inspire me on a regular basis to be a better person.

To the Cross Point staff team—The past ten years have been the ride of my life. I love and respect each one of you so much. I'm unbelievably grateful for your ceaseless encouragement, partnership, and prayer. So thankful to be a part of this team.

To Shannon Litton and Maurillio Amorim—I have no doubt that I wouldn't be writing books today if it were not for the two of you. You guys are absolute proof that just because you're behind the scenes doesn't mean you're not important. You two have been a constant source of energy, ideas, and dreams, and I'll be forever indebted for your belief in me.

To Angela Scheff—Thank you for sharing your gift of words with me and, most important, this book. Your generous and helpful contributions have made me a better writer.

To Candice Watkins—You are helpful in a thousand ways. You go above and beyond on a daily basis, and I couldn't do what I do without you!

To my entire team at Thomas Nelson—Matt Baugher, Debbie Wickwire, Emily Sweeney, Kristi Johnson, Stephanie Newton, Adria Haley, Tom Knight, and the entire amazing sales team, Caroline Green, and Andrea Lucado. Thank you, guys, for believing in me and giving me an incredible platform to share this message.

NOTES

CHAPTER 4

1. Katherine Martin, *Those Who Dare: Real People, Real Courage and What We Learn from Them* (Novato, CA: New World Library, 2004), 275.

2. Dietrich Bonhoeffer, *Life Together: Prayerbook of the Bible* (Minneapolis, MN: Fortress Press, 1996), 111.

CHAPTER 6

1. Angie Smith, *Mended: Pieces of a Life Made Whole* (Nashville, TN: B&H Publishing Group, 2012).

CHAPTER 7

1. A. W. Tozer, *The Knowledge of the Holy* (New York, NY: HarperCollins, 1978), 1.

2. C. I. Scofield, *The Scofield Reference Bible* (New York, NY: Oxford University Press, 1909), 1241.

CHAPTER 9

1. Kevin DeYoung, *Just Do Something* (Chicago, IL: Moody Publishers, 2009), 47.

CHAPTER 10

1. Henry Nouwen, *Bread for the Journey: A Daybook of Wisdom and Faith* (New York, NY: HarperCollins, 1996), 12.
2. Ronald Rolheiser, *The Shattered Lantern: Rediscovering a Felt Presence of God* (New York, NY: Crossroad, 2005), 163.

CHAPTER 11

1. Lewis Smedes, *Forgive and Forget: Healing the Hurts We Don't Deserve* (New York, NY: HarperCollins, 1996), 23.

CHAPTER 12

1. David Sheff, *All We Are Saying: The Last Major Interview with John Lennon and Yoko Ono* (New York, NY: St. Martin's Griffin, 2000), 132.

CHAPTER 14

1. Brennan Manning, *Ruthless Trust: The Ragamuffin's Path to God* (New York, NY: HarperCollins, 2010), 5.

ABOUT THE AUTHOR

Pete Wilson is the founding and senior pastor of Cross Point Church in Nashville, Tennessee, a committed church community that he and his wife, Brandi, planted in 2003. Born and raised in Nashville, Pete earned his bachelor's degree in communications from Kentucky Western University and attended seminary at Southern Seminary in Louisville, Kentucky. After planting his first church in Kentucky, Pete and Brandi returned to his hometown of Nashville to start Cross Point, a city where they felt connected with the culture as well as the people.

Over the course of eleven years, Cross Point has grown to reach more than five thousand people each weekend through its five campuses located around the Nashville area, and online. As one of the fastest growing churches in America, Pete's ministry— an outreach focused on helping people become devoted to Christ, irrevocably committed to each other, and relentlessly dedicated to reaching those outside of God's family with the gospel—has made Pete a frequent speaker at national and international church conferences.

Pete's desire to share outside of Cross Point is fueled by his love of leading right where he is. "Everything else is a natural overflow of my love for serving the local church," Pete says. With his mix of strong leadership skills and an authentic passion for Christ, he has moved into a leadership position even amongst his peers, recently being touted as the "prototype of a Catalyst leader." A strong believer in the fact that God has always used imperfect people to do amazing things, Pete inspires others to pursue God's plan despite their brokenness.

For his congregation, Pete is a loving pastor, emotionally generous communicator, and approachable friend. These characteristics easily translate when Pete speaks around the country and throughout the world and are apparent in his writing.

Pete gained national attention in 2010 when Thomas Nelson published his best-selling book, *Plan B*, a title that has been printed in five languages and launched *Putting Plan B Into Action*, a 6-week DVD curriculum that serves as a study companion to the book. *Empty Promises*, Pete's much-anticipated second book, focuses on the human desire to find purpose and hope in things that are not God. By writing honestly and transparently, Pete looks to help the reader identify their own inclination to drift toward putting their identity in other things and offer them a wake-up call to find their meaning in Christ alone.

Pete is also an avid blogger (www.withoutwax.tv); he enjoys the outdoors, fly fishing, and Titans football. When he's looking for rest, you can often find Pete working in his garden, hanging out with Brandi, or playing outside with their three boys.